SUSANNA MOODIE: VOICE and VISION

SUSANNA MOODIE

VOICE and VISION

Carol Shields

Borealis Press
Ottawa, Canada
1977

Published with assistance of the Canada Council

Cover Design by LePhan

2 1, 692

Borealis Press Limited
9 Ashburn Drive
Ottawa, Canada, K2E 6N4
Printed and Bound in Canada

CONTENTS

Special thanks to

Wanda Storto

For Don whose love and encouragement cannot go unrecorded.

INTRODUCTION

In recent years, as the study of Canadian literature has received greater attention, there has been an attempt to give the literature both historic perspective and formal shape. Survey studies have appeared in which the prevailing direction of writing in this country is examined and, to some extent, explained. These summations are, of course, extremely valuable, but a certain amount of distortion is inevitable, and one of the figures who appears to have suffered in the broad analysis is Susanna Moodie.

Mrs. Moodie, a writer of poetry, fiction, and sketches during the middle decades of the nineteenth century, is looked upon by some as the mythic figure of the anguished immigrant who embodied the alienation and neuroses of a whole nation. In her *Journals of Susanna Moodi*, Margaret Atwood writes that she was drawn to the character of Mrs. Moodie because she saw in her a microcosm of what was to become the Canadian character, what Atwood calls a "violent duality," a national split-personality consumed by a love-hate relationship with a land of freedom and hardship.[1] Too neurotic to play the role of earth-mother, Mrs. Moodie is often reduced to the role of microcosmic, schizophrenic citizen. To others Mrs. Moodie is a spoiler, an educated woman, snobbish and dour, who carried to the land of opportunity a baggage of already corrupt literary mannerisms. Ronald Sutherland, writing in *Second Image*, even questions the assumption that Mrs. Moodie was a pioneer at all. She may have roughed it in the bush, he says, "but only to a certain extent. For she was seldom reduced so low as to be without a servant and a good liquor supply."[2]

A nagging problem in an examination of Susanna Moodie's work is the inevitable conclusion that she was not, by any evaluation, a great writer, and Robert McDougall in his introduction to *Life in the Clearings* (1959) cautions readers not to lose sight of this important fact.[3] Mrs. Moodie's real value lies neither in the quality of her writing nor in her position as national microcosm; it rests instead in her historic perspective and almost singular viewpoint.

1

It is true that she often writes well, but, paradoxically, when she is being consciously literary she is furthest away from her powers. When she believes herself to be writing at her finest she is more often indulging in explosions of piety, outbursts in praise of nature, or commonplace moral speculation. Her best writing occurs in unselfconscious spells, chance remarks, sentences dropped in mid-air, blurts of belief. It is the quiet, almost thrown-away observation, the unique idiosyncratic detail, and the unwitting disclosures which mark her as a writer of accomplishment.

In order to see Mrs. Moodie in perspective it is important to remember that she was not primarily a writer; she was a Canadian pioneer, a wife and mother who happened also to write. Thus, she is reticent and understandably reluctant to sacrifice her position in society by blatant personal declarations. Though her subject material often rises from the centre of her experience, her manner of expression is usually ornate, elaborately and maddeningly private, and frequently more meditative than urgent.

In addition, Mrs. Moodie was a commercial writer; she wrote for money. She once declared that, had circumstances been different, she would have preferred to have been published without payment, but this is exactly the sort of effusion which one must eye warily. It contradicts everything else known about her: her practicality, her businesslike approach to daily life, her brisk and unapologetic concern with the cost of articles and the task of getting ahead in the world. Mrs. Moodie wrote for money, and because she was paid by the foolscap page, her work is often stretched out of shape, padded with philosophical asides, and larded with stories within stories; these devices, occasionally charming, almost always detract from the design of her work.

Her most frequently employed style is an uneasy rotation of Old World florid romantic and a New World how-to-survive handbook prose of the sort her sister Catherine Parr Traill used so successfully in her *Canadian Settlers Guide* (1855). Mrs. Moodie alternates one style with the other, writing a lyrical aside to moonlight in one paragraph, then plunging immediately into a technical discussion of logging in the next. But when she is writing close to her own experience, particularly in *Roughing It in the Bush*, consciousness of style frequently gives way to a vivid and rewarding immediacy.

A critic of Mrs. Moodie's work is quite soon brought face to face with the extreme modesty of her own expressed ambitions. In her youth she may have had higher ambitions for she confesses in a letter to Mary Russell Mitford that "A desire for fame appears to me almost inseparable from an author. . . ."[4] But her book about life in the Canadian woods was, she says, written for the practical purpose of enlightening other would-be immigrants. *Life in the Clearings* was written in response to a specific request from her London publisher, and she herself says of it:

> My book is written more with a view to convey general impressions, than to delineate separate features (LC 283).[5]

> . . . what I do know I will endeavour to sketch with a light pencil; and if I cannot convey much useful information, I will try to amuse the reader; and by a mixture of prose and poetry compile a small volume which may help while away an idle hour, or fill up the blank of a wet day (LC xiv).

Her story *Richard Redpath* (1854), she explains to her readers, is meant only to be an afternoon's diversion, and her other fiction seems designed as the same sort of harmless escapism.

Except for Mrs. Moodie's two Canadian books, almost all her other writing is set in England and aimed at an English public, and thus, those who look to Mrs. Moodie for content and style which is uniquely Canadian will be disappointed. She began her writing life as an English poet, submitting poems to English periodicals and in 1831 publishing a book of verse entitled *Enthusiasm*. Later, like her sister Catherine, she also wrote children's fiction, improving stories for young boys and girls. Indeed, many of the themes from this early genre are carried over into her mature fiction; and one of her most consistent themes, the feminizing and gentling of male strength, is foreshadowed in her children's tales such as *The Little Prince* and *Amendment* (1828).

3

Mrs. Moodie was particularly attracted to the prose sketches of the Berkshire writer Mary Russell Mitford, and her correspondence with Miss Mitford may suggest her early ambition to explore the form.

The sketch, which was very popular in the early nineteenth century, relied on a delicate tone, a familiar style, and a highly detailed texture which emphasized the charm of rural life. Quiet contemplation, country walks, regional traditions, and a dense scatter of portraits of eccentric and colourful characters all formed the content of the genre.

Mrs. Moodie's shorter sketches in *Roughing It in the Bush* follow the familiar path from reflective opening to quiet comment, but she often enlarged and to some extent fragmented the form; for she was fond of both essay and autobiography and had a distinctive didactic urge as well; these elements transform some of the chapters of *Roughing It in the Bush* from pastoral sketches to a form which was Mrs. Moodie's own creation. Thus, Mrs. Moodie's two Canadian books, *Roughing It in the Bush* and *Life in the Clearings*, are distinguished in this study from her fiction. This is not to say that large portions of the Canadian books are not fiction. They do, in fact, contain many of the elements of fiction, elements which are combined with biographical sketches, general information, and personal philosophy. They differ substantially from Mrs. Moodie's novels in intention and in the greater personal participation of the author. Carl Ballstadt points out in his essay on Susanna Moodie in *Canadian Literature* [6] that Mrs. Moodie was unable to resist projecting herself into the scenes she describes. Her own unique vision interested her more than a generalized philosophical overview, and her own interaction with local characters absorbed her more than characters viewed in isolation. Many of the sketches in *Roughing It in the Bush* are expanded into more distinctively dramatic presentations in which she used dialogue rather than description to give regional flavour and to establish the social index of her characters.

The reader who has been patient with Mrs. Moodie's ups and

4

downs of style and her lack of serious purpose, and irritated at her discursive or didactic turns, may be further discouraged by the apparent lack of unity in her Canadian books. Her work has a disturbing disconnectedness, as Margaret Atwood has pointed out, and this random quality presents some difficulty to the sensibility of modern readers.

R.D. MacDonald, in his essay "Design and Purpose,"[7] suggests that there is a sense of unity given by Mrs. Moodie's representations of nature. But in this it appears that he may have been misled by the frequency of these references and by the fact that they are distributed with marked evenness throughout all her writing. The regularity of natural-religious observations and the even patterning of them in her work seem to indicate that, rather than being a unifying characteristic, they are more in the nature of pure artifice.

Many of these nature-God references are injected into her prose without transition or explanation, and they may just as easily be plucked out without destroying the progression of the piece. The artificiality of the nature passage is also reinforced by the sort of language Mrs. Moodie employs, for she is at her most formulaic when she addresses Mother Nature or God: "How the mind expands with the sublimity of the spectacle, and soars upward in gratitude and adoration to the author of all being" (RB 28). Even the direction of her voice suffers an abrupt shift from reader to nature-deity, further accentuating the superficiality of the insertion.

This is not to say that Mrs. Moodie is not genuinely inspired by nature or concerned with Christianity. But it is misjudging her to assume that her references to nature or religion are much more than ornamental. Pious asides were part of the tradition of women writers of Mrs. Moodie's period. Jane Austen frequently paused for a moment of reverence; Miss Mitford, so admired by Mrs. Moodie, often halted her sketches with a paragraph which was half prayer and half spiritual information; even the independent Anna Jameson in her *Winter Sketches and Summer Rambles* occasionally stops and makes a ritual nod of obeisance to the God-Nature of Wordsworth.

Clearly, for Mrs. Moodie, the territory of nature and religion existed apart from the real world. At one point, when she has broken off her prose account to pay tribute to God's handiwork, she says, "But I have wandered away from my subject into the regions of Thought, and must again descend to common workaday realities" (LC 30). This distinction between the world of "Thought" and the real world is interesting for the separation of concepts and because Mrs. Moodie's language sharpens with originality when she enters what for her is the real world. In this instance, for example, she goes on to tell a series of anecdotes, three of them using dialogue which is both realistic and vigorous.

Her theology appears to be a diluted Wordsworthian passion in which religion and nature are sometimes equal or nearly equal in importance, and sometimes blended into one truth. She is more equivocal about her occasional flirtation with spiritualism. As a child she and her sister Catherine read old copies of *The Astrologers Magazine* and puzzled over the signs of the Zodiac. Catherine Parr Traill even writes in her introduction to *Pearls and Pebbles* (1894) that "Had we lived in the days of 'spiritualism' we would have been believers in its mysteries." [8]

Mrs. Moodie's nature-God-spirit trinity is cloudy, but her religious outbursts are frequent, punctual, and conventional, regular enough to suggest compulsion rather than passion. Only occasionally does Nature-God affect one of her characters directly, and when it does it is more comforting than inspiring, hinting more at psychological rather than spiritual energy. Occasionally an aside to nature sets the mood of a piece as in her chapter on the fire in *Roughing It in the Bush*, but on the whole the nature references work against the unity of the books, being interruptive, disconnective, and requiring a shift of rhetoric and tone.

A unifying force which has greater validity and which can be traced in her novels as well as her Canadian books, is the overriding sense of her own personality. For despite her reticence and privacy, she projects a vigorous sense of herself; every scene is filtered through her sensibility; every character encountered is studied in context with herself. And through the lens of her active personality,

6

one can chart a number of constantly recurring themes.

Her largest theme is the complexity and variability of human personality. The texture of eccentricity which she explored in her sketches is reinforced by her Canadian experiences, and the contradictions of human behaviour rise above mere eccentricity into something approaching mystery. Even her fiction, which on the whole is peopled with type characters, contains a scatter of strange personalities whom she cannot classify or sum up. Her own personality through which she examines her characters is constantly shifting; and in her two books on life in Canada, she assumes a tough and humourous persona. The expansion and contraction of that persona is without a doubt unconscious on the part of Mrs. Moodie, and perhaps for that reason it is of particular interest in the study of her writing.

A second consistent theme is the opposition and interaction of male and female roles. Almost all of Mrs. Moodie's works have one minor woman character of masculine habits, and always she is both laughed at and admired by the author. Her more important women characters have the appearance of genteel ladies but a strength and resourcefulness which is generally associated with male behaviour. Invariably these women are the initiators of action, the guardians of morality, and the saviours in times of disaster. Mrs. Moodie's male characters, on the other hand, are almost always weak, often overtly feminine or, like John Lindsay, a character in one of her novels, cast in the sexless role of protector. The men in Mrs. Moodie's books are continuously going through a process of feminizing; they become progressively weaker, less able to act, and more willing to be saved by women. Mrs. Moodie's book *Roughing It in the Bush* may, in fact, be read as a series of portraits of failed upper-class gentlemen settlers.

A third theme which runs through all of Mrs. Moodie's writings is a debate about the nature of society, the jig-saw puzzle into which she must fit her human oddities. She originally perceived the social structure as something fixed, but as she became more accustomed to North American life, Mrs. Moodie grew more fluid in her views. She

7

never advocates complete equality, but her discussions with herself skirt the edges of republicanism. A rather unattractive racism forms part of her world view, but it is a flaw which, when viewed in the context of her time, is no more than part of the group consciousness. She saw education as the great leveller, but emigration as a more rapid exit out of a rigid society; and her support for emigration represented, in an almost Christian sense, a second beginning.

These three themes — personality, sexual reversal and society — appear in all her writings and rise naturally from the facts of her biography. Born in 1803, she is intellectually attached to the preceding century, a century in which portraiture and interest in personality reached a crest in the writings of Alexander Pope. Subsequently the Romantics, with their introspection and respect for individualism, focused on the thousand variations and mysteries of the human personality, would exert their influence.

And she was no stranger to sexual ambiguity. Her own father failed physically and financially, and her husband's career with its accidents, financial miscalculations, and scandal was a series of disasters. Mrs. Moodie belongs to the vigorous post-Waterloo age rather than the Victorian period; women of that time were active in reform circles, and many of them, including Anna Jameson and Susanna Moodie's older sister Agnes, were beginning to make names for themselves both in literature and in the declaration of their independence.

Mrs. Moodie's social views, never very doctrinaire, derived from the simple and conventional social patterns of a pre-Reform Bill England where the shock waves of the French Revolution were still being felt and where one's station of birth was a matter of considerable importance. She herself was tormented by social dislocation; for, although her father had been wealthy, the family money was drawn from trade. And when that fortune failed, the family was placed under the double yoke of poverty and respectability. The uncertainty about the exact lines of social demarcation undoubtedly made Mrs. Moodie more open to the radical republicanism which she met in the New World. Her ambivalence and lack of polarity make her all the more valuable as a witness, an admirable and never-for-a-moment disinterested observer in the great democratic experiment of Canada.

NOTES

1. Margaret Atwood, *The Journals of Susanna Moodie* (Toronto: Oxford University Press, 1970), p. 62.

2. Ronald Sutherland, *Second Image* (Toronto: New Press, 1971), p. 35.

3. Susanna Moodie, *Life in the Clearings*, ed. Robert L. McDougall (Toronto: Macmillan, 1959), p. xi.

4. The Rev. A.G. L'Estrange, ed., *The Friendships of Mary Russell Mitford as Recorded in Letters From Her Literary Correspondents* (London: Bentley, 1882), I, 206.

5. Unless otherwise specified, quotations from *Roughing It in the Bush* are from the 1962 edition, McClelland and Stewart Ltd., Toronto. Quotations from *Life in the Clearings*, unless otherwise specified, are from the 1853 edition, Richard Bentley, London. Quotations from major works will be abbreviated in this study as follows: *Roughing It in the Bush* (RB), *Life in the Clearings* (LC), *Flora Lindsay* (FL), *Mark Hurdlestone* (MH), *Matrimonial Speculations* (MS), and Roland Massingham (RM).

6. Carl Ballstadt, "Susanna Moodie and the English Sketch," *Canadian Literature*, No. 51 (Winter 1972), 32 - 37.

7. R.D. MacDonald, "Design and Purpose," *Canadian Literature*, No. 51 (Winter 1972), 26 - 31.

8. Catherine Parr Traill, *Pearls and Pebbles* (Toronto: Wm. Briggs, 1894), p. x.

CHAPTER I

Mrs. Moodie and the Complex Personality

Flora Lindsay, Mrs. Moodie writes of one of her heroines, "delighted in the study of human character" (FL 133). And in speaking of Flora she might just as easily have been speaking of herself. Despite the fact that she often hid her absorption in personality behind the screen of nature and religion, the power and mystery of personality emerges as her overriding concern. Personality in all forms — amusing, ironic, or tragic — appears to have been her greatest diversion, and it is by examples of human personality that she attempts to divert her readers. Even when she is viewing machinery at the agricultural show in Toronto, her thoughts turn to the anonymous inventor: "True, the metal is but a dull agent, but the spirit of the originator still lives in it . . ." (LC 315).

In her book *Life in the Clearings* she describes a local circus. "People of all rank are there; and the variety of faces and characters that nature exhibits gratis, are far more amusing to watch than the feats of the athlete" (LC 97). Finding circuses boring on the whole with their repetitive clown acts, Mrs. Moodie is more amused by the sly salesmanship and coy flirtation of a candy-seller who, eyeing his wares and the pretty girls at the same time, says, "How sweet they are" (LC 97). The carnival of real life is clearly more interesting than the parody of life performed by showmen.

Describing the city of Kingston, Mrs. Moodie rushes the reader through a list of civic attributes, not forgetting to note that the trees are reminiscent of a European city, and then admits, "I must own that I felt a greater curiosity to see the convicts than the prison which contained them . . ." (LC 208). "My chief object . . . was to look at the celebrated murderess, Grace Marks."

11

Personality, individual or collective, is her major theme; but what frees her work from the commonplaceness of the character sketch is her concern with enigma, the extreme personality, the unfathomable, the complex, the personality which refuses to break down under analysis.

The study of personality was not only a source of pleasure, but a means of diverting attention from real problems. She begins one chapter in *Life in the Clearings* with a searing description of her own homesickness in the new land, but the tale of the even more unfortunate Michael Macbride dispels her gloom entirely (LC Chapt. XI). *Life in the Clearing* ostensibly is structured around a boat trip from Belleville to Niagara and the pointing out of various churches, graveyards, forests, and mills, but Mrs. Moodie performs this task perfunctorily, preferring to save her real energies for her stories about people. On the journey she is forced below to the ladies' cabin at night, and it is at this precise point that her narrative loses its random meandering tone. The women below have more to say than the sunset on the water. She advises her readers, "If you open your eyes to see and your ears to hear all the strange sayings and doings of the odd people you meet in a steamboat, you will never lack amusement" (LC 199).

In her lust after human oddity, she is relentless and sometimes indecently curious; only the extremity of the illness of Michael Macbride causes her to cease her probing. She writes how she once permitted a servant to attend a funeral on condition that he return home early and do his work. He was late, but her anger was turned aside when she saw that he had a story to tell. "My curiosity was excited." she says. "I pushed the tea-things from me and told Bell, my maid, to give James his supper" (LC 256), and, as if at a signal, both she and the reader sit back to feast.

Compared to the characters in Mrs. Moodie's Canadian books, the personalities in her fiction are often mere instruments in a plot. Uncle Beaumont in the story *Waiting For Dead Men's Shoes* (*Matrimonial Speculations* 1854) is vulnerable, comic, and picturesque with his fortune, his gout, and his love of food, but he never exhibits any of the complexity with which Mrs. Moodie describes those in her Canadian books. In her Canadian characters, Brian and Malcolm, for instance, there are blurred edges, the suggestion that it is not always possible to sum up human personality. Brian and Malcolm are not part of a story but are stories in themselves.

Many of the personalities she describes have the sketchy offbeat quality of newspaper stories or local scandals. Random and pointless, they clutter her narrative, and even Mrs. Moodie seems to sense that they are inappropriate. In *Life in the Clearings*, for instance, she tells an irrelevant story about an Irishman who reformed his cranky neighbour, a man who slit his neighbour's pig's leg, and had his own pig's mouth cut ear to ear in return. The story is awkwardly introduced with "Speaking of pigs . . ." and is concluded with a not very convincing piece of justification for its inclusion (LC 323f).

It is relatively easy to separate those stories which are hearsay from those which Mrs. Moodie has experienced firsthand. Obeying her autobiographical urge, she intrudes into many of her own stories, gladly taking a part and often the most important part. Even when she stands in the background, the reader is aware of a rush of sympathy toward the character she is describing. Uncle Joe's merriment in *Roughing It in the Bush* is disarming, and for all his rascality and drunkeness, Mrs. Moodie says that she was "taken in by him, without offering the least resistance to his impositions" (RB 92). Her visit to the lunatic asylum is described in a rush of half-formed portraits (LC Chapt. XV); what brings them together is her own excitement in discovering human qualities in those most pitiful individuals.

In those stories which she has obviously collected second-hand, she frequently signifies distance by assigning another narrator or by devising a dialogue which excludes herself. Physical details are strikingly absent, and so is the almost cinematic quality she evokes when she has actually witnessed such a scene as the prison of Kingston or the lunatic asylum at Toronto. But most telling of all is her plunge from the salty, almost colloquial descriptions of human activity to the conventional rhetoric which is the mark of her fiction. *Life in the Clearings* with its much greater second-hand content is a more subdued and formal book that the lively and autobiographical *Roughing It in the Bush*.

Perhaps the most appealing aspect of Mrs. Moodie's descriptions of human personality is her all-embracing acceptance of human variety and the infrequency of her moral judgments. Criminals, the most deviant of human beings, fill her with exhilaration rather than disgust. The "study" of human behaviour, as she calls it, includes all extremes of humanity, even the simple and the insane. The inmates of the asylum amuse her by their ironic self-misrepresentations, and she sees madness not as a horror, but as an alternative human response.

In *Roughing It in the Bush* she tells an amusing if somewhat pointless story about the shrewish wife of an innkeeper who treated her ungraciously, but, in fairness, Mrs. Moodie has to agree that she was provided a good, quick, and cheap meal (RB 45). This fairness in Mrs. Moodie's stories is like a gracenote, saving even her minor characters from crude caricature.

It is indicative of Mrs. Moodie's overriding concern with the complexities of human personality that she is unable to sustain an abstract argument without illustrating it, frequently to the point of imbalance. For instance, in *Life in the Clearings* (Chapt. VIII) she launches into an attack on the social custom of wearing mourning, beginning with a brief discussion of the foolishness of mourning from a religious standpoint. "It is not a reproach to Him" (LC 175), she asks, when all nature is in a perpetual state of change? From the religious reference she hastens through the philosophical arguments to the social argument which interests her far more and which she illustrates with a total of eleven anecdotes. These stories, some of them fragmentary and some of them crisply detailed, over-argue the case so emphatically that the reader suspects they exist for their entertainment value alone. Her best anecdotes are those in which irony is the controlling mood as in the story about a woman who

14

orders her mourning clothes before the expected death of her brother and then is disappointed when he lives through his illness (LC 183f).

Human detail outweighs the literary framework in Mrs. Moodie's Canadian books; the framework, in fact, can be accommodated to hold any number of stories. One can look at three chapters in *Life in the Clearings*, the story of Michael Macbride (Chapt. XI), the story of Jeanie Burns (XII), and the stories of the lost children (XIII); all these stories happened years before the Niagara journey, but Mrs. Moodie has no apparent difficulty inserting them into the scheme of *Life in the Clearings*. She simply begins her chapters with a mention of where she is on her journey and remarks that she is reminded of a story. Her transitions tend to be either fragile or crude, and sometimes even non-existent, but she seems not in the least reluctant to interrupt her design with a sketch from human nature.

The chapter on work bees in *Roughing It in the Bush* (Chapt. 13) is typical of a series of short, disjointed human anecdotes grouped under a chapter theme. Mrs. Moodie disliked bees, considering them a necessary evil in frontier life. The only redeeming feature was the opportunity they afforded to view an odd assortment of humanity at a glance and to study the interaction of personality. Temperance men such as her brother and husband are dismissed quickly. It is the more offbeat guests who engage her: old Wittals who combined a speech defect with a gross appetite ; an illiterate but amazingly successful revival preacher; John who is unrivaled at the art of swearing; the slightly but not obnoxiously drunken Malachi Chroak who foolishly pretends to force one of the maids into marriage. All these sketches are slight; they seem to have been written from notes and suggest an awe for human variability rather than individuality.

But Mrs. Moodie's curiosity is also excited by characters viewed in isolation; she is detached, almost scientific at times, offering little which might be considered judgmental on individual human irregularities. Writing about a farmer's wife listening to a story about

15

a doll who could actually speak, Mrs. Moodie says, "It was amusing to watch the expression of surprise, wonder, and curiosity that flitted over the woman's cadaverous face. She would have made a good study for a painter" (LC 200). Another example of this sort of surreal flash which interests her is the young man whom she sees playing his pipes to the animals on board ship. She expresses delight at his lusty performance, as though she had swept the crowd with her gaze and picked out the one ironic element. When she passes an island and is told that a hermit lives there, she declares, "I was very curious to obtain some particulars of the private history of this eccentric individual (LC 205).

Eccentricity, which Mrs. Moodie not only tolerated but relished, is most frequently attached to the upper-class and appears in her work to be, almost without exception, a male indulgence; women were too occupied, apparently, to stray from the conventional path for long, and as for the poor, such deviations in behaviour were more likely to be viewed as barbarous and ignorant than tolerably eccentric. Some of the eccentric personalities described by Mrs. Moodie are so extraordinary that she feels compelled to supply a supporting footnote. On page 202 of her novel *Flora Lindsay*, she writes about one individual, "A fact." And on page 226 she writes a confirming note — "This touching scene was witnessed by the author."

Gentleness usually accompanies the variety of eccentricity she describes, and her human oddities are often kind to the point of aberration. Wilhelmina Carr in *Flora Lindsay* is expansively generous, and Tom Wilson in *Roughing It in the Bush* betrays a curious sweetness beneath his eccentricity. Even Malcolm, who was irritable and rude most of the time, was fond of children and gentle on occasion. And in almost every case of rampant eccentricity, Mrs. Moodie outlines her personalities with loneliness and suffering. Eccentrics such as Brian, Tom, and Malcolm in *Roughing It in the Bush* are not reduced by Mrs. Moodie to comic size; instead they contain their separate afflictions like species of private pain.

In her Canadian books Mrs. Moodie describes countless acts of eccentric and ironic behaviour. But her novels and tales, on the other hand, contain far more interchangeable characters, and personality is more likely to hinge on gender than on personal anomalies. Occasionally, though, her fictitious characters show complexities beyond their role type, and Mrs. Moodie herself, in a discussion of fiction , states her belief that a writer must blend qualities of good and evil in a character in order to make him believable (LC Chapt. XIV).

William Mathews, for instance, who is a minor character in Mrs. Moodie's novel *Mark Hurdlestone*, is a fairly generalized representation of criminal low life. But he has periods of complexity in which he lapses into feelings of guilt. Mrs. Moodie even supplies him with something like a psychological explanation for his behaviour: the loss of his mother, Mathews says at one point, has flawed his life. Cruel and uneducated, he has strange pockets of sensitivity. When his father dies he says, "Something is gone — a string is loosened from the heart . . ." (MH 201). Unlike Godfrey, his partner in crime, William is haunted by conscience. Dark, frightening visions torment him, a voice from the "shut up depths" of his heart (201). Pursued by the law, he is also pursued by "blue devils that pinch and freeze my heart" (201). William speaks with a kind of dark poetry which places him in contrast to Godfrey, but, disappointingly, Mrs. Moodie does not develop his personality further; instead she allows him to harden along criminal lines.

In much the same way, Roland Massingham, the chief character in the novel of that name, is more than just another bad boy; he is driven by mysterious compulsions, and he says at one point, "I love to have my own way, and feel as it were compelled to resist the control of others" (RM 144). "I cannot bear to see another person in action and myself standing still."

In *Mark Hurdleston*, the leading character is greatly simplified by Mrs. Moodie at first. He is the unmitigated consummation of evil: "There was not a drop of human kindness in his composition" (MH 4), Mrs. Moodie tells her readers. He "never" mingled; he had "no"

17

friends; "no one" had ever shaken his hand. But later his character receives some psychological shading: he is not the personification of wickedness; instead he is mad. He hates women. He is cold and unresponsive. He has a fetish about cleanliness and a mania about gold. He has distinct paranoic symptoms: he believes people are trying to poison him or gain knowledge of his wealth. And he has what Mrs. Moodie hints might be an unnatural relationship with Grenard Pike, a being just as strange in his own way as Hurdlestone.

The Green sisters in the story *The Miss Greens* (MS) are introduced as highly stereotyped spinster sisters, and one of them, Lydia, never becomes more than a vain, weak creature, an indolent sipper of brandy. But Polly Green, obviously Mrs. Moodie's favourite just as she is the favourite of the suitor, develops into someone more recognizably human. She even has stirrings of wit; she makes her prayers short, she says, to repay the stinginess of Providence. And though she claims to be no philosopher, in her limited way she is. "Love," she says, "at the best is but a weakness, that the fondest grows ashamed of" (MS 129). John Andrews, returning from his midnight courtship, admits to being half-captivated by Polly. But she never progresses beyond this interesting and contradictory point, and Mrs. Moodie leaves her as a bride, shamefully abandoned at the altar. The whole story, in fact, is marred by a viciousness on the one hand and a heavy-footed irony on the other.

The characters in *Richard Redpath* (MS) are mainly stylized and conventional. Joshua Baynes, a foolish gourmand, and his daughter Betsey (who grieves when her fiance is drowned because her wedding clothes will be out of fashion before another groom is found) are both without real substance; even Mrs. Moodie doesn't pretend to take them seriously. But the character of Benjamin Levi is confusing, incomplete, and mysterious. Levi is a Jew, but even this status is confused for he terms himself a convert. His profession is not clearly defined either; he is both an editor and a seller of second-hand clothing. Robert Redpath, when first hearing about him, says, "he has a thousand counterparts in our great metropolis" (MS 225).

18

But the others tell him that he is mistaken, that "there is a mystery about the man, something about him unlike other men" (225). Levi, they claim, was "sent among us as a punishment for our sins" (228). Popularly considered to be sly and cunning, Levi is a natural philosopher, a cynic in the Shylock manner, given to such paradoxical declarations as "I never vouch for the truth of a story . . . until I know it to be a lie" (235). It may be that Mrs. Moodie had originally conceived a more ambitious role for Levi, but in a weak conclusion she has him suffer an absurd humuliation and death while her less interesting characters crow with glee. Obviously fascinated with Levi's contradictory personality, Mrs. Moodie has difficulty assimilating him into her fictional world; Levi, like Hurdlestone and William Mathews, is a human oddity who exists on another level of reality.

The reader gets the impression that Mrs. Moodie is unconscious of the contradictory natures of some of her characters. Aunt Dorothy in *Mark Hurdlestone* is one of these unwittingly complex people; she has all the standard equipment of a tart and a witty spinster, but her hatred of men and her contempt for romance have an edge which goes beyond the limits of her conventional role.

Mrs. Moodie's interest in personality is more than passive. She is, by her own frequent admission, a student of human behaviour, and it goes without saying that she interests herself in the motivation behind behaviour. Not surprisingly, she often demonstrates the pre-Freudian prejudices of her time. She is content to dismiss the crime of Grace Marks (LC, Chapt. X) as an inexplicable visitation of sin. And she takes careful note of the phrenological evidence she sees at the prison in Kingston. She has, in addition, a strong romantic belief in the human countenance as an "index" to the mind. "The human countenance never lies," she says in *Mark Hurdlestone* (24); one must learn to trust one's first impressions. But Mark Hurdlestone, like Malcolm in *Roughing It in the Bush*, has a deceptively strong face; it is necessary to look closely and with discernment in order to see the cruel mouth and the cold eyes.

Occasionally Mrs. Moodie explains personality behaviour as

19

the result of occult interference. John Andrews in the story *The Miss Greens* is visited in his dream by his dead wife who persuades him to alter his course. And Jane Redgrave in Mrs. Moodie's serialized story of that name (1848) dreams on her wedding night that she will meet disaster.

Mrs. Moodie is a woman of her times who quite naturally reflects current ideas about personality, but often she suggests psychological motivation as well. Brian, the still-hunter, she speculates, has a retarded son whose affliction may be the root of Brian's melancholia. Malcolm, her unwelcome guest, may have acquired his irascible disposition from uncaring parents. In the novel *Flora Lindsay*, one of her later works, Mrs. Moodie frequently takes the trouble to supply causative factors for personality aberration. Captain Kitson, a neighbour of Flora's, has accumulated his eccentricity through a lifetime of social non-acceptance. Mrs. Ready owes her aggressive vulgarity to a too rapid shift from lower to middle class. Wilhelmina Carr, one of Mrs. Moodie's most extraordinary characters, provides a rapid oral sketch of her life in which many of the seeds of her later bizarre behaviour can be found; her mother had died at her birth, and her stern absentee farther had been a figure of fear and dislike. Her stepmother, herself a victim of class dislocation, had indulged her, and her schoolmates had jeered at her physical oddities. Furthermore, the only man she had ever loved had refused her offer of marriage, and the only child she had been drawn to had abandoned her.

Early influences, Mrs. Moodie seems to feel, are permanent and almost impossible to overcome. Algernon, the brother of Mark Hurdlestone, is early introduced to extravagance and pleasure by his effeminate uncle, Alfred, and these vices "clung to him through life" (MH 19). Frequently personality is shaped by a parent's favouritism or neglect, and Mrs. Moodie explains the nature of Armyn Redgrave by the fact that his mother had favoured his brother. Mark Hurdlestone was a favourite of his father, while his brother Algernon was a favourite of his mother, a situation which not only influenced their characters but damaged their relationship with each

20

other. And the psychic shockwaves were felt from one generation to the next: Algernon, Mrs. Moodie says, became a "fatally indulgent father" (MH 75) to his son Godfrey.

Her random and off-hand psychological speculations are sometimes startlingly modern and sound. When Marcella DeTrueba in the story *Richard Redpath* contemplates suicide, she is advised by an old seaman that suicide is no more than a means of punishing someone else; this piece of wisdom is reinforced by a story he tells of his own daughter's suicide. Clearly Mrs. Moodie subscribes to this theory because Marcella instantly recognizes the truth of it.

Aside from describing the motivation behind personality, Mrs. Moodie reveals her characters through combinations of physical description, use of incident and dialogue, shifts in narration, and direct comparison through the mechanical pairing of characters.

Her fictional characters are described in a formulaic manner, but those characters she introduces in her Canadian books are frequently brought to life in a few words. A lecturer on mesmerism whom she meets in *Life in the Clearings* is sketched in a way which blends his somewhat supernatural appearance with his twanging charlatanism.

> Imagine a tall, thin, bearded American, exhibiting himself at a small wooden desk between two dingy tallow candles, and holding forth in the genuine nasal twang of half-supernatural sciences . . .
>
> (LC 98)

In *Roughing It in the Bush* Old Joe's mother is presented with a strong portrait sense. When she is visited by Tom Wilson, the old woman is seen busily shelling cobs of Indian corn into a barrel (RB 88). There is a completeness in the description which not only expresses her personality but sets a scene. In the next chapter Mrs. Moodie discovers the woman in her cottage "shelling white bush-beans into a wooden bowl" (RB 96). Again there is the pictorial quality, the insistence on details, a suggestion of industry which makes a footnote to the old woman's personality.

21

With no more than a sentence or two Mrs. Moodie picks out various guests at a working bee: "Lieutenant _____ in his blouse, wide white trousers, and red sash, his broad straw hat shading a dark manly face that would have been a splendid property for a bandit chief" (RB 156); "Levi, the little, wiry, witty poacher"; "Cornish Bill, the honest-hearted old peasant with his stalwart figure and uncouth dialect" (RB 159). Apart from physical details Mrs. Moodie is an observant and sensitive reporter on the nuances between people. One night, intercepting a look between two subjects who were pretending to be mesmerized, she says, "I shall never forget the sidelong knowing glance he cast across the bench to a friend of his . . ." (LC 99f).

As in her chapter on bees in *Roughing It in the Bush*, Mrs. Moodie frequently gathers together a number of related anecdotes, interspersing them with comments on society. Writing about the charivari or the Yankee custom of borrowing, she clusters several stories together, each one forming a single snapshot image of a group attitude. The looseness of the form permits her to shift the narration when she chooses: sometimes she tells the story herself, sometimes a friend relates it, and sometimes the story is overheard. Many of these stories use dialogue as in her discussion with Uncle Joe (RB Chapt. 7), a skill she doubtless developed as a writer of children's fiction, and sometimes the dialogue is set up formally as in an actual play; Chapter 6 of *Roughing It in the Bush* when Tom Wilson confronts the old woman is a good example.

Many of these grouped stories give only the slightest insight into human behaviour, but occasionally Mrs. Moodie is able to encapsulate a personality in a rapid series of incidents. The chapter on the servant John in *Roughing It in the Bush* (Chapt. 8) is shaped almost like a short story. The scene before his arrival is carefully set, his actual entrance is dramatically presented, and the elements for farce are set into motion when the servant girl learns that she must spend a night under the same roof with a Papist. Clearly, though, this chapter is meant to be an examination of a complex personality whom Mrs. Moodie regards with obvious affection. For John, so

22

poor that he has neither shoes nor socks, feels that he possesses the soul of a gentleman. His parentage is uncertain, permitting him to fantasize about wealthy parents, fine clothes, and money. His essential willingness to be helpful, as when he tries to make maple sugar or to wash his shirt, is thwarted by curious flashes of ineptitude. John, a helpless but charming dreamer, moves from incident to incident, and emerges memorable if not resolved.

One chapter of *Life in the Clearings* (XIII) strings together four stories, all of them about lost children, and it is interesting that Mrs. Moodie uses a narrator when she might just as easily have told the stories herself. The narrator in this case is a Mrs. H._____, "a woman whose husband farmed our farm on shares" (LC 270). There is a hint of the lower class about Mrs. H._____; more importantly, she is a Canadian, ignorant of English niceties. The different narrator gives Mrs. Moodie an opportunity to speak authoritatively about the problems in the New World without sounding presumptuous. It also permits the narrative to be flavoured with sentiments and endearments: "These little chaps are the sons of a poor emigrant who came out" (LC 270).

In revealing personality, Mrs. Moodie has a modern interviewer's knack for asking the right question, inquiring of Brian "what made him so fond of hunting?" (RB 125). She quotes his reply quickly and simply, using the verb "said" in these dialogues, a device Hemingway used much later to focus the reader's attention on the words of the reply. The chapter on Uncle Joe and his family (RB Chapt. 7) opens with a dialogue between Joe and Mrs. Moodie, and there is a reportorial quality to the scene as Joe betrays his character through his words. Mrs. Moodie's part in the conversation is purely that of questioner. "How did the change agree with him?" she asks. "And had the whiskey nothing to do with this change?" (RB 93).

It is Mrs. Moodie's use of dialogue which does more than anything to relieve her discursive heaviness. When she attempts dialect, which she does frequently in her Canadian books, there is more than a suggestion of condescension, but when she catches regional expressions or subtle class differences, she conveys character concisely and accurately. On ship for Niagara in *Life in the Clearings* she observes and describes a group of seasick women, wives of farmers and mechanics. Though she remarks that "the language they used was neither very choice nor grammatical" (LC 201), Mrs. Moodie provides a sense of their separate personalities through snatches of dialogue. She has a special ear for speech which is typically Canadian, noting that when Canadians discuss death; their attitudes are reflected in their choice of words. "My brother's death has been looked for these several months past," one woman says (LC 171). And a man, roughly declining an invitation, says, "No, can't — much obliged; but I'm afear'd that grand-father will give the last kicks while I'm away" (LC 171).

In instances where personality is not clearly marked, particularly in her fiction, Mrs. Moodie employs a traditional means of revelation, that of comparing paired personalities. When male characters are being compared in this manner, the twinning is both frequent and fairly rigidly adhered to. The two brothers theme in *Jane Redgrave* is typical: Armyn and Edward Sternfield are brothers competing for their mother's attention. In true Cain-Abel pattern, Armyn is eventually responsible for Edward's death. Even Mrs. Moodie's short pieces, a story from the *Victoria Magazine* entitled "The Son of Arminus," for instance, use this shorthand device for the comparison of character. [1] In this story one brother is cast in the role of hero while the other, a traitor, suffers guilt. In the novel *Roland Massingham*, Roland is first paired off with his sister Anne who is outwardly meek but morally strong, the diametrical opposite of Roland who is physically strong but morally weak. Later Roland is paired with his brother Robert who possesses a greater moral strength and endurance and who, symbolically, replaces Roland in the surgery. Roland's mother, by way of example, tells a story about her two brothers Myles and Frederick. Myles was doted upon by his mother, and Frederick, neglected and hostile, killed Myles in a hunting accident. The Redpath brothers are also offered as comparisons in personality and so are the Green sisters.

But the best example of twinning is found in the novel *Mark*

Hurdlestone. The comparison apparatus is elaborate and consistent; three generations are, in fact, paired and compared. Squire Hurdlestone is contrasted with his weak brother Alfred. The Squire's two sons, Mark and Algernon, differ sharply in character, and each of them has a son, Anthony and Godfrey, respectively. The structure is best seen in diagram form.

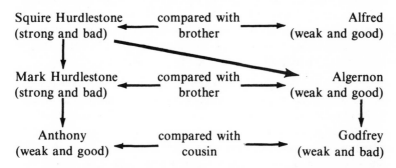

Squire Hurdlestone   compared with   Alfred
(strong and bad)   brother   (weak and good)

Mark Hurdlestone   compared with   Algernon
(strong and bad)   brother   (weak and good)

Anthony   compared with   Godfrey
(weak and good)   cousin   (weak and bad)

The use of pairing of characters to point up personality is less rigid when women are concerned. Women are usually seen in larger groupings, confusing the comparison, and, furthermore, they relate to each other in more subtle ways, sometimes even crossing class lines and forming a flank. The women in *Mark Hurdlestone*, for example, include the first Mrs. Hurdlestone, an ill-defined shadowy creature who acts in secret against her husband. Her daughter-in-law Elinor is a solitary woman who, despite her basic goodness, is victimized by men. Juliet, Mary and Clarissa, the final generation, mingle their separate strengths to form a rescue team for the unfortunate Anthony.

Most of Mrs. Moodie's character revelations seem to be consciously formed from a combination of description, incident, dialogue, and comparison; but in the case of John Lindsay, the husband of Flora Lindsay, the personality is revealed, seemingly unconsciously, in his actions and speeches. Indeed, the narrator ironically insists that John Lindsay is a perfect gentleman. His strength and talents are praised repeatedly, but, in contradiction, his essential heartlessness is revealed again and again. He can't be bothered taking Flora's old nurse to Canada, and even as he is kissing Flora's tears away, he is turning her to his advantage. When she "begged . . . entreated . . . coaxed" him to go on an outing with her, he bluntly refused (FL 136). Mrs. Moodie puts into his mouth speeches which make him a cruel manipulator. He wins his wife to his side in the argument over immigration by shaming her and making her feel she has been ungrateful. His attitudes are fixed and brutal and he has no tolerance for eccentricity; he is a relentless realist in combat with Flora's romantic nature. "I hate mystery in any shape" he tells Flora with finality (FL 6).

Flora, on the other hand, even as the narrator insists that she is an obedient wife, shows a willingness to experiment; she has an easy relaxed tolerance and an active curiosity. She is also more intuitive; had the Lindsays followed Flora's plan of not taking a servant to Canada they would have been better off. Flora's decision on which ship to take was also, in the end, the wiser course.

Flora and John are compared in their attitudes and reactions, but one senses that, though Mrs. Moodie may be consciously making a heroine of Flora, her vilification of John Lindsay is unconscious. And it is interesting and tempting at this point to make biographical conclusions, for if Flora is a simplified extension of the author, John is almost certainly a counterpart of John Moodie, Mrs. Moodie's difficult husband, a stubborn man who was not particularly likeable or fortunate in personal dealings.[2]

Indeed the character sketches in *Roughing It in the Bush* have one common link: most of them, at least the best of them, are of failed upper-class Englishmen — Tom, Brian, Malcolm, and always, hovering in the background, the shadow of Mr. Moodie himself. They constitute a type which Mrs. Moodie is able to represent dramatically, for in each case there is a sense of inevitability. Goodness is defeated, intelligence is scorned, sensitivity is clouted. The proper equipment for life in the bush, Mrs. Moodie seems to be saying, is ignorance, brute strength, and an absence of preconceptions.

Uncle Joe, Mrs. Moodie's neighbour, and Jacob, the English servant, are examples of the sort of men who survive in the woods. Joe has a wily rascality which passes for strength, and Jacob, who lived with the Moodies for some time, has many of the qualities which for Mrs. Moodie epitomized the English working class. He embodies the childlike graces which Wordsworth assigned to the working poor: he is honest, pious, impulsive, and natural. When he shoots a buck with a single shot, thereby providing the household with much needed meat, he credits Providence rather than his own skill. Jacob is densely bucolic; he has a round rosy face suggestive of fresh air and good milk, and he possesses the yokel's inarticulateness. The scene in which he proposes to the serving maid is presented in dialogue which Mrs. Moodie shamelessly admits to overhearing. Jacob's love speech is delivered in cloddish blurts; his kisses are audible, and his dialect is stage comic at an almost bovine level (RB 174f). Mrs. Moodie describes him as a "kind-hearted creature," and shows him "sobbing" out his good-bye to the family. "Jacob's attachment to us," she says, "in its simplicity and fidelity, greatly resembled that of a dog" (RB 173). But Jacob, Mrs. Moodie clearly indicates, is the sort of simple man who has a future in the new country.

It is quite the opposite with Tom Wilson. If ever a man was predisposed to fail as a pioneer it was Tom. Mrs. Moodie may have intended her remarks on Tom to be no more than a sketch of a colourful eccentric, but the terrible seriousness of his mental affliction comes through and overshadows his comic aspect. It may be that the symtoms she describes were less alarming in the nineteenth century than they are today; in any case her attitude toward Tom is one of total affection and acceptance of the person he is, however peculiar. And as with the lunatics at the asylum, her view of him precludes any thought of change or improvement. Though some of Tom's responses are clearly mad — for instance, his mistaking day for night — she touches only passingly on the possibility of madness, preferring to call him one of "nature's originals." "You might suspect his sanity," she writes, "— a matter always doubtful — but his honesty of heart and purpose never" (RB (50).

Tom Wilson was so extraordinarily complex that Mrs. Moodie is called upon to invent a vocabulary and imagery to describe him. He is the "very prose of prose" (49). He is famous for his "nothing-to-doishness' and "seemed afraid of moving about for fear of knocking his head against a tree, and finding a halter suspended in its branches — a man as helpless and as indolent as a baby" (49). But Tom has a darker, paranoic side. He has a horror of mingling too intimately with his fellow passengers, a fear so strong that he hires an extra berth to ensure his privacy. He chooses not to travel with the Moodies because, as Mrs. Moodie says, "He was afraid that my baby would keep him awake of a night. He hates children, and says that he will never marry on that account" (58).

And yet, for all his oddity, Tom has a current of common sense. His remarks on the subject of emigration are only too prophetic. He warns John Moodie that a gentleman will never be able to work as a labourer. And he cautions Susanna Moodie that her bookish ways may alienate her in the new land. Many of his droll remarks are sharply epigrammatic, betraying a shrewd intelligence at the bottom of his muddled brain. Asked how he entertained himself during a boring lecture, he replied, "By thinking how many fools were collected together to listen to one greater than the rest" (53). Mrs. Moodie's gentle retelling of Tom's history, amused and affectionate, says much about her own personality. And yet, Tom Wilson is one of the few characters whom she does not use to lever her own persona into fuller view; when Tom is concerned, she is willing to step aside.

Of all Mrs. Moodie's personality sketches none is more shapely than the portrait of Brian, the still-hunter (RB Chapt. 10). The reader senses that the unsolved riddle of Brian's madness forms an exceptional attraction for her. Brian's story begins with a sudden dramatic meeting; there is a flashback about his life narrated by another visitor, and then there are several incidents concerning Brian, each a miniature portrait, each more fully illustrative of his complexity. There is even a monologue in which Brian attempts to explain his life.

Mrs. Moodie is less interested in the cause of his malady than she is in the effect, although she does once suggest that Brian's son's disability may be partially responsible. Brian is a man who is torn apart by ironies: he has several times attempted suicide but is afraid to cross the ocean for fear of drowning. He loves life but finds pleasure in killing. He has caused many of the settlers to fear for their lives, but he brings a message of comfort to Mrs. Moodie. He himself is capable of responding to irony, marvelling that a visiting naturalist should prefer the simple weeds to the lovely flowers. Brian says of the naturalist, "Well he was an innocent man . . . a very little made him happy . . ." (RB 134). Mrs. Moodie repeats this statement as a double irony, for this is the way she actually sees Brian himself. The chapter on Brian ends a little too rapidly with a hasty note on Brian's later suicide and an equally hasty tribute to his goodness, but one senses that the unfinished edge to the sketch proceeds from Mrs. Moodie's own inability to comprehend the most thrilling and impenetrable of her characters.

"Human nature," Mrs. Moodie writes in *Roughing It in the Bush*, "has more strange varieties than any other menagerie can contain, and Malcolm was one of the oddest of his species" (190). Malcolm, the stranger who forced himself on the Moodies for a period of nine months, is described in the chapter "The Little Stumpy Man." He may be the most complex of all the characters Mrs. Moodie describes. The chapter about him is even more fragmented than her usual writing; she jumps from episode to episode in her frustration with him. She is plainly baffled. The string of anecdotes succeeds in forming a multi-lensed portrait of him, but the portrait is never finished; even Malcolm's eventual disappearance is clouded in mystery.

Usually razor-sharp in her physical descriptions, Mrs. Moodie falters with Malcolm. She is self-contradicting, calling him unpleasant looking, but testifying to his regular features and good colour. His voice is low and mysterious, and she senses that "the current of his feelings seemed to flow in a deep sluggish channel . . ." (178). The cumulative effect of the description suggests sexuality, and this impression is strengthened as Mrs. Moodie circles around Malcolm, drawing sometimes closer, sometimes further away.

29

Malcolm's tendency is to be unkind and rude, but in odd moments of intimacy he confesses to self-hatred and perpetual melancholy. In one extraordinary exchange he confesses to Mrs. Moodie that he has murdered a man. Mrs. Moodie receives this confidence with remarkable calm. Suggesting neither trauma nor untruth, she simply adds the murder episode on top of the pile of mysteries. When Malcolm mentions a miserable boyhood, an ill-natured mother, and a brother who was insane, she makes no link between these revelations and Malcolm, the misanthropic adult.

But she herself is more clearly revealed in this chapter than in any other place. Malcolm does not hesitate to tell her she is a prude, and Mrs. Moodie does not hesitate to repeat the charge. He also tells her that he is a man who thinks with his head, not his heart, implying perhaps that she is just the reverse. These personal exchanges between Malcolm and Mrs. Moodie are a real departure from her usual pattern; she is neither the shrewd interviewer nor the unseen observer, but a participating human being who has let her persona slip. She is often angry with her guest, petulant, bored, fascinated, exasperated, wounded, and, in the end, mystified, perhaps as much by herself as with Malcolm.

Margaret Atwood sees Mrs. Moodie as a woman divided down her Victorian middle, all manners and ladylike art forms on one side, and on the other a consciousness of sweat, dirt, disease, and mosquitoes.[3] But it is possible that the dichotomy is not rooted in Mrs. Moodie's personality; it may be only a surface splintering, a division which exists for literary purposes, namely the division between person and persona. Her real and vulnerable self is only occasionally glimpsed; it can be seen in her conversation with Malcolm or unwittingly expressed in her selection of anecdotes and characters. Approaching Canada for the first time she confesses to an emotional seizure: "it was not fear but a sort of nerving of my spirit to meet the worst."[4] She once refers briefly to the tragic drowning of her son, and there are oblique, scattered references to anxiety, weakness, and ennui, what may have been a nervous collapse near the end of her sojourn in the woods. But these are exceptions, slips of the pen, holes in the persona which she constructed for herself.

Carl Klinck suggests in his introduction to *Roughing It in the Bush* that Mrs. Moodie has "touched up" her characters in order to enlarge her own personality (RB xiv). Certainly she chooses characters who by their brutality and coarseness magnify the shock to her own sensibility in the New World. And there is a noticeable absence of women of education and sensitivity beside whom she might have shone less brightly.

Her persona in her early works is that of romantic heroine, the adventurous, felicitous spirit which reached fulfilment in the person of Flora Lindsay. Mrs. Moodie likes to show herself counselling servant girls, healing the sick, teaching the infidel; she is the generous, humourous, resourceful deliverer as in the chapter "The Walk to Dummer" in *Roughing It in the Bush.*[5] She is proud of her ability to be resourceful and she expresses that pride in ironic terms, the irony being that she, a woman of gentle breeding and education, should now be making coffee with dandelion roots and producing rows of well-hoed potatoes. When she fails in her first bread baking, Tom Wilson says, "I hope you make better books than bread" (RB 90). She replies that she would rather fail as a writer than as a baker, but she is really suggesting the opposite: she is a gentlewoman to whom the mysteries of the household are unknown. Her exploration of domesticity is deliberately childlike, a pose which reinforces the image of herself as a woman of culture.

Her sensitivity to nature, she frequently points out, separates her from other people. When she marvels at the beauty of the St. Lawrence, she is conspicuously alone at the rail; her fellow immigrants are unconcerned. Later, visiting Niagara Falls, she compares herself with a local woman who is indifferent to the sight. Mrs. Moodie, on the other hand, insists several times that she is overwhelmed by the view. Her initial homesickness in Canada is lifted when she encounters the countryside. "It won me from my melancholy and I began to look around me with considerable interest" (RB 68). But her English servant, she points out, does not

31

have the ability to be lifted from sadness by scenery. A positive response to nature signified for Mrs. Moodie a delicacy of taste, an educated sensitivity.

In meeting her new countrymen she contrasts the paucity of their knowledge with her endless fund of facts. She believes that her health is nourished by fresh air, and she eats fresh apples although others tell her not to. She is the keeper of knowledge and the foe of ignorant superstition. Her persona is expanded and reinforced by the fact that she is often vicitmized by rude borrowing neighbours or scorned by the illiterate for her bookishness. Her uniqueness is stressed by her isolation, and her isolation is increasingly insisted upon as she moves from *Roughing It in the Bush* to the more reflective *Life in the Clearings*.

Her vision of herself as a heroine in an ongoing drama is stated most openly in the chapter "The Burning of the Fallow." [6] In this episode she and her family have narrowly escaped death by fire; at the very moment before destruction a thundershower saves them. Later she learns that the scene has had one chance witness, an Irishman who had watched from a distant canoe. For reasons which she doesn't even attempt to explain, she finds the fact of having had a witness "comforting." It is as though her role-playing is reinforced by the existence of an audience. Her own persona, so patently constructed and so elaborately expanded, would otherwise have dissolved, unwitnessed and unverified, in the backwoods of Canada. From this innocent disclosure, one arrives at the conclusion that all of Mrs. Moodie's writing may have represented an attempt to find confirmation of her existence, an existence which was hidden in an alien wilderness and all but buried alive.

NOTES

1. Susanna Moodie, "The Son of Arminus — A Tale of Ancient Rome," The *Victoria Magazine*, No. 4 (1847; rpt. Vancouver: University of British Columbia, 1968), pp. 77 - 82.

2. For a revealing self-portrait of John Moodie see the Introduction to his book, J.W. Dunbar Moodie, *Scenes and Adventures as a Soldier and Settler* (Montreal: subscription printed by John Lovell, 1866).

3. Margaret Atwood, *Survival* (Toronto: Anansi, 1972), p. 51.

4. Susanna Moodie, The *Victoria Magazine*, No. 3, 68.

5. Susanna Moodie, *Roughing It in the Bush* (London: Richard Bentley, 1852), Chapt. XII.

6. *Ibid.*, Chapt. III.

CHAPTER II

Mrs. Moodie and Sexual Reversal

The Canadian experience was a liberating one for Mrs. Moodie. Though she accepted her landscape as inevitable, she found, mainly through her writing, the means to overcome its natural restrictions. She was not insensitive to the comparisons between cultures, nor did she ignore the changing social conditions of her time. Her work, in fact, reflects the times, moving from her early moralizing, sentimental tales to sketches which reflect a broader, more generous acceptance of life.

Nevertheless, a panoramic look at the writings of Susanna Moodie uncovers one rather startling feature: the women figures in her work tend to be strong, moral, and aggressive, while the males, almost without exception, are weak, easily corrupted, and malleable. Furthermore, the interaction of males and females frequently leads to the progressive feminization of men and the elevation of women to the position of rescuer.

This theme, however, is never openly stated, and it may be that Mrs. Moodie uses the pattern unconsciously. She was, of course, not unaware of liberal ideas about marriage or women's rights; more than once she defends spinsterhood as an honourable and even enviable state. And her own life bears witness to the fact that women could rise to prominence. But her view of the social structure and her position in it were rigidly prescribed. In her books the overriding narrative tone is modest and maidenly, taking for granted a fixed view of sex roles. It is only in the working out of individual destinies that the reader becomes aware of a subtle and consistent sex war in which the reversal of the prescribed order is the rule: men are victims of society and women are victors.

34

Superficially conventional about sex roles, Mrs. Moodie falls into ritual female phrases when discussing her husband's desire to emigrate, allowing him a "superior mandate" (RB 137), and she herself answering the "command of duty." She was capable of calling her husband by the cliché "my better half," all the while perhaps entertaining doubts as to the truth of the term. In her writings Mrs. Moodie makes a pretext of following her assigned role as a member of the less able sex, and in so doing she parrots some of the sexual biases of her time. In *Life in the Clearings* she remarks:

> Women make good use of their eyes and ears and paint scenes that amuse or strike their fancy with tolerable accuracy; but it requires the strong-thinking heart of man to anticipate events, and trace certain results from particular causes. Women are out of their element when they attempt to speculate upon these abstruse matters — are apt to incline too strongly to their own opinions — and jump at conclusions which are either false or unsatisfactory.
>
> (LC 283f)

Interestingly, despite this disclaimer, she proceeds to offer her opinion on the future of Toronto and other social concerns which catch her interest (LC 282). And in her division of sexual aptitude she is far from being negative about the female side; the female is accurate and amusing, she says, and perhaps more feeling. Her attempt to separate and examine sexual patterns is reflected in her many Canadian observations. In *Life in the Clearings* she talks about a woman's right to talk in a certain way (LC 5), but mentions that a woman cannot speak out on such things as political problems (52). Ladies in Canada, she writes, are served first at dinner, the men standing until the ladies have finished and gone to the drawing room. Frequent comments such as these on the division of male and female activities underscore the importance Mrs. Moodie attaches to gender.

It is important to bear in mind that in pioneer days in Canada, particularly in times of trouble, roles were frequently reversed, and

Mrs. Moodie refers to these experiences with a nonchalance which suggests familiarity. When she gave birth to her third child in the midst of an epidemic of summer fever, her serving man Jacob cooked, baked, and churned "as carefully as the best female servant could have done" (RB 165).

The ability to shift the sexual role was to her commendable; when it involved a simultaneous shift in social level it became more difficult. In 1835 the Moodies were too poor to pay the wages of a hired man, and Mrs. Moodie was forced for the first time to work in the fields. "I had a hard struggle with my pride before I would consent to render the least assistance on the farm . . ." (RB 166), she writes. But she became accustomed to the blurred roles which farm life demanded, and she speaks with pride of her five-year-old daughter who could manage a canoe and catch small fish.)

Mrs. Moodie was an observer of the manifestations of sex roles and she was also a thinker, though perhaps not a very original one. The first chapter of *The Miss Greens* is, in fact, a discourse on the subject of spinsterhood. Women, she writes, accept the first offer of marriage for fear of being ridiculed as old maids. In effect they commit an act of "legalized prostitution" (MS 82). By accepting spinsterhood gracefully, Mrs. Moodie believed that a woman might fulfil the role of "female philosopher" (80). Certain women, she continues, are by temperament unsuited for marriage, but the contempt of the world for old maids forces these women to adopt ridiculous artifices in the hope of snaring a husband. These absurd creatures turn themselves into "everlasting flowers."

Mrs. Moodie's book *Matrimonial Speculations* contains a group of three long stories, and their unifying theme, superficially at least, is the tragedy which results from contrived marriages. There are several debates about the advisability of marrying for love or money, but the central plea which Mrs. Moodie almost unconsciously expresses is that a woman may, without losing honour, elect not to marry. Mrs. Moodie, perhaps with Miss Mitford in mind, is invariably impressed by examples of feminine independence. She quotes a contented widow she meets in Canada as saying, "I like to have my own way — to lie down a mistress and get up a master."[1]

Mrs. Moodie presents women as having a natural predilection for good. With anthropological thoroughness she compares the numbers of male and female prisoners in the Kingston penitentiary and concludes that women must have superior moral training. In fact, their instinct for goodness may be natural: the first Mrs. Hurdlestone naturally and instinctively favours Algernon over the sinister Mark.

Men, even good men such as Algernon, are easily corrupted and destroyed. Women, on the other hand, even when tainted or exposed to sin, are not corrupted; instead their dilemma more often leads to breakdown, insanity, and occasionally to suicide. Mary Mathews in *Mark Hurdlestone* has several fits of insanity as the result of her pregnancy, and Elinor has a serious breakdown after her tragic marriage. Madness is Mrs. Moodie's short cut solution to the problem of the victimized female. Jane Redgrave, after a forced marriage and the loss of her baby, goes quietly insane for a period and so does the nurse in Flora Lindsay after the drowning of her lover. Mrs. Moodie herself may have been no stranger to mental instability; in *Roughing It in the Bush* she hints at anxiety and depression, and in *Life in the Clearings* she undertakes a therapeutic journey for an undisclosed illness.

In Mrs. Moodie's books men preempt for themselves the province of eccentricity, the world of practical jokes and rough pleasure, but, at the same time, they are more often involved in tragic situations. Women feature in anecdotes as being ignorant and easily shocked, but it is men whom Mrs. Moodie finds ridiculous. Mr. Grove from Peterborough, a young farmer who comes to call in *Roughing It in the Bush*, is clumsy, meticulous, and vastly comic. In Jacob's courtship scene with Mary, he is the buffoon, she the cool manipulator. Malcolm is a pitiable man; for all his coarse brutality, he is a baby who must be flattered, listened to, and agreed with. Women, while not always independent, are mutually supportive. It is a woman, a Mrs. O _____, who comes to comfort Mrs. Moodie and her servant girl when they are frightened of the charivari. Mr. Moodie, as almost always, was absent.

A number of biographical factors may account for the preponderance of strong female figures in Mrs. Moodie's books. Her father failed her, first by losing his fortune and then by losing his health. It was her mother who held the family together and whose letters and parcels sustained the Moodie family in their bush cabin. In Mrs. Moodie's family, the Strickland sisters outnumbered the brothers five to two, and all the girls in the family were given a liberal education. Her most famous sister, Agnes, remained financially independent all her life; and Catherine, her sister who emigrated to Canada, married an older man who suffered from serious mental affliction for much of his life, forcing her to take over the management of the family.

(John Moodie, her husband, as distilled from both her writing and his own, is less than an heroic figure, a man preoccupied with social distinctions and predisposed to financial miscalculation. Mrs. Moodie herself did far more than work in the fields: she supplemented the family income by painting and writing, and she procured for her husband, without his consent, the post of paymaster to the militia. Doubtless too she played a part in his later appointment as sheriff of Hastings County. In their joint editorship of the *Victoria Magazine* he contributed only a few pieces, while she literally wrote most of the magazine herself. Although she speaks of him with unfailing fondness, as a partner in life he was almost certainly the weaker partner.)

The story *Waiting for Dead Men's Shoes* outlines Mrs. Moodie's sexual concepts so neatly as to be almost diagrammatic. Characters are set out in opposing groups. There are two houses: Dr. Beaumont presides with fumbling imeptitude over one and the widowed Mrs. Harford with grace and intelligence over the other. A third contingent is composed of two young law clerks, one cruel and conniving, the other a humble lover of beauty. After the initial personality distinctions are made, Mrs. Moodie sketches further refinements. The Harford house itself is divided by temperament.

The two sisters, Caroline and Rosamond, illustrate the opposing sides of the feminine character. Rosamond represents excessive femininity; she is all that is impulsive, giddy, volatile, and silly. Caroline, in contrast, is prudent, given to sarcasm, intellectual discourse, and dry summations. Rosamond tells her openly, "I hate your cold, phlegmatic people . . ." (MS 6). Caroline cooly defends herself with, "I say less, Rosamond, but perhaps feel more." Never very much at home with symbolism, Mrs. Moodie clumsily shows Caroline taking her tea without sugar while Rosamond helps herself to three lumps and then carelessly drops scalding water on the dog's tail.

The two suitors, Clement Cotterel and Edward Freeburn, reflect the two sides of masculinity. Edward is a brutal male, cunning and lacking in imagination, and his chief concern is to find a rich wife. (He has, Mrs. Moodie informs the reader, inherited his low disposition from his father). Clement is his reverse image, the son of worthy though humble parents, possessed of "refined feelings" and an admiration for literature. The situation of the fortune-hunting male brings a cry of outrage from Mrs. Moodie. ". . . alas, how many lovely and accomplished girls shipwreck their happiness by bringing the first pure offerings of a guileless heart, to present in fond idolatry, at such an empty shrine" (MC 24).

Of course, Mrs. Moodie doesn't pretend that all women are guileless. In *Waiting for Dead Men's Shoes* there is Mrs. Orams, Dr. Beaumont's housekeeper, who tricks the old man into marrying her. She is gross and masculine in appearance, as sly as the greedy Edward Freeburn, and she is punished in the end by sudden death from too much food and brandy. But Mrs. Orams belongs to a lower social order, and the masculine traits so attractive in Caroline, are viciously unattractive in her.

Caroline, in contrast, possesses positive and independent qualities. She boldly declares that she is thinking of working for a living and she will live happily alone if she finds no suitable spouse; and it is she who suggests the plan of emigrating. George, the brother of the two Harwood girls, is vapid and unimaginative, given to flattery and shallow thinking, and he permits others to make decisions for him. He marries a slight, feather-brained creature, and allows his sister Caroline to take them both to Canada. There is no doubt that Caroline is the heroine of the story, embodying all that Mrs. Moodie admires in a woman. She is clever and manipulative; it is she who visits her uncle and persuades him to give George a purse of money for his marriage. She is resilient and imaginative, the only one in the story who is able to express her will. Victorious to the end, she quickly finds a husband of her own choosing in Canada.

All the men in the story are weak, the weakest of them the confused and elderly Dr. Beaumont who marries his housekeeper rather than look for a new one. Like George Harford he is seemingly incapable of thinking of alternatives.

The masculine women described by Mrs. Moodie sometimes combine unattractive qualities with a sense of excitement and freedom. Mary Mathews in *Mark Hurdlestone* illustrates Mrs. Moodie's ambivalence toward emancipation.

> (Mary) was more remarkable for the beauty of her person and her masculine habits than for any good qualities . . . a man in everything but her face and figure . . . Her masculine employments had destroyed the woman in her heart. She thought like a man — spoke like a man — acted like a man.
>
> (MH 138f)

The headstrong Mary sang rude songs and made coarse jokes, but Mrs. Moodie appears to admire her reckless bucolic freedom and her natural energy. "I am my own mistress," Mary says, making both a class and a personal declaration. But she loses her independence by falling in love with Godfrey and bearing his child. Ironically it is her single feminine lapse which has destroyed her, and, insane with grief, she is saved not by Godfrey, but by another woman, Juliet.

The male-female paradox is clearly evident in Mrs. Moodie's serialized story *Jane Redgrave*. Rose, the heroine, is a sturdy country girl; she loves to run in the fields, milk the cows, and wander

40

at will. The two men she favours are both sensitive and religious to the point of piety; more importantly, both of them are physically maimed. Arthur Wilbrook, her teacher and mentor, is lame; and Edward Harlands, her lover, who weeps, sighs and faints, is a deaf-mute.

Mary and Rose exhibit Mrs. Moodie's perhaps unconscious equating of masculinity with a state of nature and femininity with the state of being civilized. Rough male qualities are more pronounced in girls of the lower social orders, and Mrs. Moodie, first arriving in Canada, is shocked as well as fascinated by the savage swearing women on Gross Island. "We were literally stunned by the strife of tongues. I shrank, with feelings almost akin to fear, from the hard-featured, sunburnt women as they elbowed rudely past me" (RB 25). Females of the upperclasses projected their strength through their good sense. Women in Mrs. Moodie's stories tend to possess money and to be good managers; men, in turn, have a tendency to covet and then squander fortunes.

Mrs. Moodie's men could and did weep openly, reflecting the eighteenth-century idea of the good man of feeling. But women are expected to keep their composure. Aunt Dorothy says to Juliet when she is weeping, "Come Miss Whitmore, you must raise yourself from this unwomanly grief" (MH 170).

The story of Jeanie Burns which Mrs. Moodie tells in *Life in the Clearings* is a good example of the strength and composure of women dominating over the weak excesses of men. In this story Jeanie is a totally admirable woman, attractive and self-sufficient. After the death of her parents, finding herself barred by custom from following the family trade of shoemaking, she survives by making waistcoats for local tailors and binding shoes for shoemakers. Eventually she sets up her own establishment, becoming nothing less than a modern day businesswoman. Willie Robertson, who loves her, sends her forty dollars to come and join him in Canada, but when she delays out of kindness to a friend, he, in a fit of rage, marries another woman. Heartbroken, Jeanie nevertheless accepts the situation of Willie's desertion and never again "breathed his

41

name" (LC 267). As Mrs. Moodie remarks, "the grief that has nae voice, like the canker-worm, lies ne'est the heart." In the end Jeanie dies, still bravely silent, and Willie's reaction is violent and in marked contrast to Jeanie's stoic control. In front of his wife he breaks down at Jeanie's grave and weeps. "And he flung himself upon the fresh piled sods, and greeted like a child" (268).

Wilhelmina Carr, a minor figure in *Flora Lindsay*, is perhaps the most sexually dislocated of all Mrs. Moodie's characters. An enormously wealthy woman, Miss Carr wears a man's hat, refuses to have servants, smokes a pipe as well as cigars, drinks brandy and gin, and "swears like a man" (FL 34). Perhaps modelled on the famous Viennese eccentric Ida Pfeiffer, Miss Carr had toured Europe on foot and alone. She wears short skirts; fashion, she believes, should be functional. She prefers conversation to needlework and says, "Women are just as able to shift for themselves as men . . ." (37). "I am gloriously independent and mean to remain so" (38). She has long since accepted her eccentricity and is unconcerned with social approval. She sees a kindred strength in Flora and tells her that with a little spirit she too could emerge as an independent woman. "I am not fond of men," Miss Carr says, "I have no reason to be fond of them" (39). Miss Carr is scornful of the conventional womanly posture of passivity, saying that "passive women are always great favourites of men . . . a vain man loves to see his own reflection in one of these domestic magnifying glasses" (44f). Furthermore, men monopolize all the good things of life. A glass of brandy, she tells Flora, is as much her right as it is her husband's. Flora's reaction to the supper she shares with Miss Carr is understandably guarded, but she is plainly exhilarated by their debate.

Jenny, Mrs. Moodie's servant described in *Roughing It in the Bush*, is less eccentric than Miss Carr but no less interesting. During the winter of the rebellion when John Moodie was away, Jenny and her mistress ran the farm like two men, even doing the sugar making themselves. Jenny served as Mrs. Moodie's protector. She was unafraid of bears, handy with an ax, inventive and cheerful. Her easygoing masculine assurance was hard won. In a chilling biography of Jenny, Mrs. Moodie shows how she triumphed over male dominance. Jenny, with her rough mannerisms, comes close to caricature, but Mrs. Moodie describes her with an affection which borders on envy.

By contrast, John Monaghan, for all his coarse appearance, is eager to assume female tasks. Mrs. Moodie seems to think it only natural that, since John's appearance caused the servant girl to leave, he should step into her shoes, sweeping the floor, nursing the baby, and even cooking the dinner. Brian, her strange neighbour, has about him certain feminine aspects as well: vulnerability and a softness which seems to appeal to Mrs. Moodie. He is fond of flowers and he loves children, sometimes surprising the family with a gift of milk for the baby.

It is a special irony that men with huge masculine frames should possess womanly fears. For instance, John Browne, the singing master described in *Life in the Clearings*, is an enormous man and so tough he can stand any amount of cold. But he is terrified out of his wits by a dog sleeping beneath his bed. In contrast, the travelling musician has a slight physique and an engaging modesty. He admits his lack of physical strength, but it is he who rescues John Browne from the dog.

Mrs. Moodie does not take the outward signs of femininity as a show of weakness. She is, in fact, quite casual about men who do household tasks. She does not condemn Alfred in her novel *Mark Hurdlestone* because he is fond of cooking, embroidery, and visiting the sick, but because he is more concerned with manners than with morals. Nor does she think it unmanly to shed a tear; on the contrary, she believes that only the most harsh form of maleness, as personified by Mark Hurdlestone, remains perpetually dry-eyed. These manifestations are acceptable to her until they merge with a larger pattern of moral weakness and physical cowardice.

The feminizing of young men figures prominently in Mrs. Moodie's writings, and even her early children's fiction deals with what was called "the breaking of a boy's spirit." In her story

Amendment (published 1828) a rebellious boy named Charles Grant, spoiled by his father, is placed under the influence of a cowboy, Giles Bloomfield. Giles is a sweet-natured lad who "reads the Bible...and nursed the baby; and is kind to his sisters."[2] Charles, under the influence of Giles, becomes tender, more spiritual, a lover of animals and nature.

Roland Massingham is a more fully-developed study of the feminization process. At fourteen Roland has all the male vices in the budding: he is headstrong, determined, domineering, and self-centred. Under feminine pressure he is gradually brought to a state of subservient virtue. His aunt Mrs. Newman scolds him for his independence and expresses her hope that he will "be guided by others instead of always relying on yourself" (28). Roland's sister Anne lectures him gently on the wisdom of love, and his mother's wise counsel eventually delivers him, chastened and weakened, to the door of the church. After much weeping, blushing, and wringing of hands, Roland becomes a humble candidate for the clergy. A symbol of his surrender is the amputation of his left hand while pursuing that most masculine of activities, hunting.

The female as advisor and reformer of the male is a constantly recurring image in Mrs. Moodie's writing, and even more common is the tableau of the upright female nursing the prone male. And it is a posture which is almost never reversed. Elinor nurses Mark Hurdlestone in his illness and even steals money to buy him medicine, this in spite of the fact that she hates him. Marcella in *Richard Redpath* tenderly nurses Henry Ingate back to strength. An even more extreme example is found in *Mark Hurdlestone* when Clarissa, dying of consumption, rises from her sickbed to minister to the stricken Anthony who collapses after his flirtation with suicide. Mrs. Moodie frequently shows herself nursing her husband or a male friend. It is an image which both literally and figuratively illustrates the weak susceptibility of men and the upright strength of women.

The device of pairing personalities is used to compare male weakness with female strength. John E——— is a particular favourite of Mrs. Moodie, and from what she writes about him, one can see that the appealing part of his nature was his very obvious feminine side. All the males in John's family were endowed with "soft, silky, fair hair and milky complexions" (RB 197). Mrs. Moodie says little about John's helping in the field; what excites her admiration is his ability with a needle. He can cut and sew his own clothes and mend his socks and shoes; he even knits for the Moodie children. In addition, he is fastidiously clean. Mrs. Moodie remarks that the only thing that made John cross was the rough work of logging; he thoroughly disliked the dirty work and would always bathe as soon as he returned in the evening, even begging a piece of the scarce household soap.

Jenny, the female servant at the time, scoffs good humouredly at his need for soap. Unlike John she loves rough masculine adventures. Twice she ventures out with Mr. Moodie on bear hunting expeditions, carrying the knife and acting as his bodyguard. She is afraid of nothing: "she snapped her fingers at the idea of the least danger" (RB 214). Jenny even tries to interest John in a direct competition in the wheat fields, a challenge which he wisely declines.

In the story of Michael Macbride in *Life in the Clearings* Mrs. Moodie shows an extraordinary contrast between mother and son. Michael's Irish mother is described as being masculine, ignorant, and unreasoning. "The young man seemed shocked at the unfeminine conduct of his mother, and begged me to excuse the rude manner in which she answered me" (LC 239). The dying boy, in contrast, pale and peaceful in death, is defined as a feminine presence, and like all Mrs. Moodie's feminine idealizations, he has a talent for music and a respect for the scriptures.

Uncle Joe, a drinking wastrel in *Roughing It in the Bush*, is contrasted with his old mother who is cunning and mean but always, Mrs. Moodie points out, industrious. Her ability to live alone and maintain herself wins Mrs. Moodie's grudging respect.

The history of Grace Marks in *Life in the Clearings* is told from the point of view of Macdermot, her male accomplice in crime. It is clear as the plans for the murder develop that Grace is the instigator. Macdermot, the son of respectable parents, Mrs. Moodie points out, only jokingly suggests that they murder their employer. Grace immediately takes up the idea and makes all the plans. When Macdermot's courage fails him, Grace taunts him into a mad rage. After the crime Macdermot is condemned to hang and Grace is reprieved. Macdermot says, "This seems very unjust to me, for she is certainly more criminal than I am" (LC 229). Mrs. Moodie obviously agrees, for the whole act has been engineered and set into motion by the female, Macdermot being no more than an unwilling agent.

In the chapter "The Walk to Dummer" in *Roughing It in the Bush*,[3] the story is told of Captain and Mrs. N_____ who typify Mrs. Moodie's concept of male-female strength. Captain N_____ is ruined by drink; he is corrupted not because he is bad, but because he is weak. His wife, watching her husband regress, grows in strength, single-handedly holding the family together, rationing out potatoes while at the same time maintaining the family dignity. Captain N_____ is also contrasted with Jenny who had formerly worked in his house. Jenny, unmarried, independent, strong and steadfast, had been thrown out by the crazed Captain N_____ who refused even to give her her wages. The juxtaposition of the personalities makes its point: men waste away; women endure.

Part of female strength, Mrs. Moodie suggests, springs from a more subtle understanding of human nature. In one of the charivari anecdotes in *Roughing It in the Bush*, a widow takes a husband younger than she is and is tormented night after night by a crowd of men. It is she and not her young husband who knows how to control the barbarians; she pretends amusement, then craftily issues an invitation to one of the charivari leaders, and by good humour and common sense manages to have the ongoing charivari brought to an end.

In *Mark Hurdlestone* there is a simultaneous strengthening of Juliet and a progressive feminization of Anthony. Foolishly romantic at first, Juliet grows both philosophical and independent;

46

she rides horseback and takes upon herself the tutelage of Godfrey. Anthony meanwhile weeps, faints, and moons over letters and old portraits. He enters the childlike world of Clarissa, over-reacting with her to romantic trifles. On one occasion he expresses his disappointment at Juliet's handwriting; it is bold and energetic while he would have preferred it to be elegant and flowing. He becomes unable to initiate action himself and is reduced near the end of the novel to a state of childishness, petitioning his father for help and resorting to tantrums to frighten the old man. The only positive act he can envision is suicide.

In the story *Richard Redpath* Mrs. Moodie again, as in *Mark Hurdlestone*, uses the pattern of two brothers, this time to form a masculine-feminine contrast. Richard is the stronger of the two; it was he who took the initiative in their emigration to Jamaica, and he who rebounds from the disaster of the shipwreck with spirit and resourcefulness. Robert is more indolent, a lover of books and "refined pursuits [who] shrank from any collision with the rude and vulgar . . ." (MS 168). In this story two females are also placed in contrast: there is the totally feminine Betsey who is pretty and spirited but, Mrs. Moodie explains, not overly intelligent. She is a "beautiful toy" (187), just the person to win the heart of young Richard. Betsey is contrasted with Marcella DeTrueba who is beautiful and intelligent. Marcella is not masculine in any obvious outward way, but she shows remarkable strength and independence in her refusal to make a marriage of convenience. She is a doer, a rescuer; she is active where Betsey is passive, and she allies herself with Henry Ingate, the weak, innocent young aristocrat who has accepted without question the marriage his elders have arranged for him.

The story *The Miss Greens* is dense with sexual shrubbery; the sisters are clearly a couple, Polly taking the male role and leaving the feminine, the ugly side of femininity in this case, to Lydia. Polly croaks and growls while Lydia screams, whimpers, and shrieks. It is Polly who takes the reins while driving the donkey cart and she who bears up to the teasing of the boys. John Andrews, their suitor, has a mixture of male and female traits. A "pretty young man" with white hands and soft golden hair, he is the son of a barber. But he prefers to call himself a hairdresser since he has "a natural taste for genteel society" and prefers the "soft tresses of young girls" to the "stumpy beards" of men (106).

Maggie Grant and her husband Tam, described in *Roughing It in the Bush*, make a mini-portrait for the whole male-female arrangement. Tam has carelessly left the boat at Quebec and fallen in with whiskey-drinking friends; he doesn't catch up with Maggie until several days later. When they are reunited she is loving and forgiving, and Tam promises not to repeat his folly. But Mrs. Moodie remarks that she would not be surprised if Tam were led astray again.

Tam and Maggie, while accepting the dependence of the female, represent an acceptance of male weakness and its corollary, female strength. But in Mrs. Moodie's novel *Flora Lindsay*, traditional dependence is tested. The whole novel, in fact, outwardly a simple story of a family emigrating to Canada, is a subtle struggle between wife and husband for control. The stage for the struggle is set in the first chapter by the introduction of two minor characters, Captain Kitson and Mrs. Ready. Captain Kitson is a man who has taken to domesticity, usurping his wife in the kitchen and washyard. "Talk of women wearing the smalls indeed," Mrs. Kitson protests. "Captain Kitson is not content with putting on my apron but he appropriates my petticoats as well . . ." (F10). Mrs. Moodie apparently sees the captain as an extreme example of sexual reversal. Mrs. Ready, in turn, is the caricature of the aggressively masculine wife. On the topic of women who are obedient to their husbands she says, "I repudiate such passive obedience as beneath the dignity of women. I am none of your soft bread-and-butter wives who consider it their duty to become the mere *echo* of their husbands" (22).

Flora does not want her husband John reduced to the ludicrous condition of Captain Kitson, nor does she want to assume the role of aggressor; what she wants is a degree of independence and respect. At one point she tells her husband about a gypsy who told her

48

fortune, propheseying that she would marry a sea-going man and that she would wear the breeches in the family. John Lindsay laughs dismissingly at the tale, but the exchange is followed by a discussion between Flora and her husband over the choice of ship on which they will travel to Canada. In the end Flora has her way (although her husband stubbornly maintains that it is not because he is giving in to her wishes), and she is proved right in her choice; they later learn that the ship her husband had favoured had been wrecked on the coast of Newfoundland.

Flora may see her husband as an obstacle to her freedom, but she never makes a direct assault. She disobeys him by associating with Miss Carr and by going on an outing by herself, but she confronts him indirectly with a charming, teasing insolence. "We all know what a jealous monopolizing set you men are," she says. "Let anyone attempt to interefere with your rights and . . . you are armed to the teeth" (146). Her weapons are subtle and traditionally feminine, and she almost always gets her way. The story of Flora's beating the captain at draughts is a microcosm of her position; she knows the captain resents being beaten by a woman, but she cannot resist the temptation. She knows the social code and as far as she can she obeys it; when she cannot she makes what might be called a "soft" strike for freedom.

Mrs. Moodie too knew that she was not fully liberated. She was on the whole a docile wife, but sometimes her grudging attitude shows. When she and her husband landed in Quebec they heard that there was a cholera epidemic in the city. Her husband insisted that she stay on ship. "I yielded at last to the wishes of my husband," Mrs. Moodie says acidly, "who did not himself resist the temptation in his own person . . ." (RB 31). Later, when she rescues her husband from the disgrace of poverty, she does so by private letter and without her husband's consent, much as Dorothy, the heroine of *The World Before Them*, (1868) assists Gilbert's rise in the army.

A sailor in *Flora Lindsay* puts sexual roles at their most brutal: "women are made to bear — men to resist" (FL 98). Mrs. Moodie must have recognized that this was clearly the division of burden in her day, but it is interesting that the sailor makes the feminine role active while the masculine role — resistance — is passive. The myth of male dominance is subscribed to by Mrs. Moodie, but it is just that: a myth. There is little doubt where real strength resides. In all her writings there are many men who are strong, brutal, and even criminal. And there are hosts of men such as Anthony in *Mark Hurdlestone* who are good almost to the point of being angelic. But there is a significant absence of men who combine both strength and goodness. Heroism as it is traditionally understood, a combination of daring and determination, nobility and virtue, is never demonstrated by the male characters of Mrs. Moodie's works. But these same qualities occur over and over again in her women characters: in Jeanie Burns, in Flora, in Marcella DeTrueba. Heroism is the property of wives, mothers, daughters, and most of all, of the women who face life alone.

NOTES

1. Susanna Moodie, *Roughing It in the Bush* (London: Richard Bentley), II, 8.

2. Susanna Moodie, *The Little Prisoner* or *Passion and Patience* and *Amendment* (London: Newman, 1829), p. 83.

3. Susanna Moodie, *Roughing It in the Bush* (London: Richard Bentley, 1852), Chapt. XXIII.

CHAPTER III

Mrs. Moodie and the Social Structure

For all her literary wanderings, Mrs. Moodie never loses sight of the social order. And for her the social order represents far more than a backdrop for human activity; it exerts a powerful force on personality. Characters in her novels, because of their location on the social scale, respond in particular ways: the manner in which they speak and their view of the world is shaped and limited by their social position. Furthermore, dramatic effects, both comic and tragic, occur almost axiomatically when two levels of society collide, causing a fissure in the established structure. Education and emigration provided the only real escape from social bondage.

Mrs. Moodie's two Canadian books show something of the distance she was forced to travel in her social concepts. *Roughing It in the Bush* records the inevitable clash between radical democracy and the conventional social system of pre-Reform Bill England. Mrs. Moodie participated, albeit passively, in that struggle, often being the object of attack and more frequently a shocked witness to change. In *Life In the Clearings* she concentrates less on the colourful, rugged individual, and turns instead to an examination of society as a whole. It is a more mature and civilized book, less vivid in its impressions, but more reflective and much more of a summing up of her own position as an immigrant. A comparison of the two Canadian books shows how she learned to compromise, at least to a degree, with the new democracy. Her own working experiences gave her a respect for manual accomplishment, and she recognized a degree of nobility and honesty in the lower classes. Never a social egalitarian, she nevertheless endorses a more fluid social system in which intelligence, hard work, and stern morality are rewarded by the respect of society.

51

Robert McDougall in his introduction to *Life in the Clearings* calls Mrs. Moodie's social posture one of compromise, but he points out that the exact point of that compromise is not firmly fixed.[1] Although altered, her political ideas remain vague; she is easily tugged first one way and then the other. Occasionally presenting broad social theories, she almost invariably contradicts herself by an offending example. Each new personal experience had a transforming effect on her, preventing her from arriving at a fixed position in her social philosophy; her consciousness, firm on fragmented experience, fails her on larger concepts. It is tempting to sum up her social attitudes by saying, as many have done, that Mrs. Moodie's response to life was schizophrenic.[2] But it is perhaps more accurate to say that she remained open-minded, surprisingly open-minded in view of her position, her age, and the fact that she was burdened with the social contradiction of her era.

Her own social situation, of course, was confused: as a child she had belonged to a wealthy and privileged family, but her father's money had been made in trade. Later, after he lost his money, she remained an impoverished member of the middle class. As a married woman in Canada she was an educated gentlewoman, but one who was forced to take on hard manual labour. Still later in Belleville her social position was threatened by scandal. Her position as a writer conferred prestige on her, but isolated her within her own caste.

Part of Mrs. Moodie's social ambivalence sprang from her curiosity about the lower classes and the fact that her class conditioning suppressed that very curiosity. The narrator in *Flora Lindsay* talks about a self-imposed distance when she says of the dancing of the lower-class passengers on board the *Anne*, "The Captain and the Lindsays never joined the dancers; but it was a pretty sight . . ." (FL 213). This deliberate separation led to a remoteness, and, when reading Mrs. Moodie's descriptions of lower-class activities, one suspects that she is often more romantic than realistic, more stereotyped than individual. Mrs. Moodie was not, even while milking cows or tending her potato field, really in touch with that level of society.

Tom Wilson, a character in *Roughing It in the Bush*, is almost brutally realistic about the finality of class divisions. "Gentlemen can't work like labourers," he says, "and if they can, they won't" (RB 54). Mrs. Moodie herself speaks without self-consciousness of superiors and inferiors, her patriotic heart fueling her confidence in the accepted social structure. Recognizing that "Perfect, unadulterated republicanism, is a beautiful but fallacious chimera..." (LC 78), she nevertheless claims that society derives its health from a system of rank. A book review she wrote in the *Victoria Magazine* directly challenges republicanism.

> Mr. McQueen [the author] in his hatred of kings seems to forget that certain distinctions of rank, are necessary to the well-being of society. That it little matters by what name we call them — that men of wealth, talent and education will exert a certain influence over the minds of their fellow men, which would continue to be felt and acknowledged in the world, if mankind were equalized tomorrow.[3]

Wilhelmina Carr, the wealthy eccentric in *Flora Lindsay*, echoes Mrs. Moodie's dismissal of pure republicanism: "As to pure democracy, my dear, that's all humbug. No well educated wealthy persons ever consider themselves on an equality with their servants" (FL 59).

Nevertheless, the narrator in *Flora Lindsay* describes Canada as "a country destitute of a hereditary aristocracy . . . where the poorest imigrant, by industry and prudence, may rise to wealth and political importance" (31). In Canada, Mrs. Moodie writes, "The want of education and moral training is the only *real* barrier that exists between different classes of men" (LC 75f). But the mere breath of democracy can lead to instant class mobility. The narrator in *Flora Lindsay* warns that "they [servants] no sooner set foot upon the North American shores than they are suddenly become possessed with an ultra republican spirit" (FL 68).

Mrs. Moodie's social view, confused by the collision of romanticism and reality, was further clouded by her Christian moral concepts. Certainly she does not feel that there is a basic difference in moral responsibility between the classes. Discussing the foolishness of wearing mourning in *Life in the Clearings*, she says:

> If it becomes a moral duty for the rich to put on black for the death of a friend, it must be morally necessary for the poor to do the same. We see no difference in the degrees of moral feeling; the soul of man is of no rank, but of equal value in our eyes whether belonging to rich or poor.
>
> (LC 187)

Frequently Mrs. Moodie makes an attempt to put her ambivalent feelings into formulaic terms. By the time she wrote *Flora Lindsay* she had lived in Canada for many years, long enough to have considered some of the social differences between the old world and the new.

> The aristocracy of England may be divided into three distinct classes — that of family, of wealth and of talent . . . the one which ranked the last should hold its place with the first, for it originally produced it; and the second, which is far inferior to the last, is likewise able to buy the first . . . In Canada the man of wealth has it all his own way.
>
> (FL 32)

Mrs. Moodie, always clinging to the English idea of rank, ascribes to the gentleman certain physical refinements which make him instantly recognizable. When Marcella discovers the half-drowned Henry Ingate on the beach in *Richard Redpath*, her first words are, "What a fine countenance! This surely must have been a gentleman" (MS 207). Marcella indicates that rank is her first concern for she had not at that point discovered whether Henry is alive or dead. Beautiful and intelligent, Marcella is the idealized portrait of a woman, undoubtedly reflecting Mrs. Moodie's own values.

Class has a strong connection with profession as well as birth. In the story *The Miss Greens*, Kitty Lilack, the milliner, refuses to marry John Andrews until he agrees to convert himself from a barber into a corn merchant. Levels within levels are indescribably subtle, but certain rules are inflexible: "A shopkeeper was but a tradesman despite his independence," Mrs. Moodie sums up in *Richard Redpath* (MS 168).

Besides birth and education, a certain apparently inherent strength of character is attached to the upper class. When John Andrews in the story *The Miss Greens* declares that he will follow his young wife to the grave by fasting, Mrs. Moodie remarks with finality that "Englishmen in that class cannot fast long" (MS 109). Godfrey in *Mark Hurdlestone* enters the lower criminal classes when he is desperate, but even then he does not relinquish all his gentlemanly ideals: he expresses genuine shock when William Mathews strikes his own sister. And in *Roland Massingham*, Jacob's drunkeness is excused with the tacit acknowledgement that he is only a servant and, thus, not accountable. But Roland, who is of better class, has greater moral culpability; he is punished for giving Jacob the money which led to his drunkeness.

Manners and speech are often the key to class, and Mrs. Moodie, by the use of ungrammatical dialogue or speech laced with regionalism, pinpoints a character's position in the social scheme. In the sentence "He got his wife Peggy — or my Peggy as he called her . . ." (RB 158), she clearly sets out the man's social and educational level in the briefest possible way — the word "my," as in "my Peggy," being an instantly recognizable class clue. Many of Mrs. Moodie's linguistic observations were gleaned from watching the reactions of servants, and in *Flora Lindsay* the narrator explains that "The mistress who in England was termed the *dear lady* now degenerates into *the woman*" (FL 68). Servants, newly initiated into the middle class, adopt the titles and airs of the aristocracy, a situation which Mrs. Moodie finds hilarious. But it is principally through her servants that Mrs. Moodie is able to observe the workings of democracy.

Some of Mrs. Moodie's social observations are casually mentioned, revealing the almost instinctive way in which she categorized the various levels of humanity. About a little lost girl, she remarks that she had a "sagacity beyond her years and not very common to her class . . ." (LC 275). At other times she is consciously defensive as in the Introduction to *Mark Hurdlestone* when she gives a spirited if somewhat tedious discourse on the current state of Canadian letters. She would like to write without payment, she says, but cannot afford it. But, she says, manual labour is not to be despised; how else can one understand the working man. Occasionally Mrs. Moodie's social observations are given in a tone of ringing declaration. "The grief of the lower orders is generally loud and violent" (MH 22). But in making this allusion to Mary Mathews in *Mark Hurdlestone*, she equates expression of this sort with a direct natural response and is less condemning than awe-stricken.

Mary Mathews is, in fact, one of the few to speak out against the injustice of her station. She hates Juliet Whitmore as much for her class as for taking her lover; indeed, she sees these two things as one. Her own easy morality is also explained by her as a class phenomenon. It is pride, she says, that keeps fine ladies like Juliet from sexual laxity. Mary's social ideas though, however forceful, are roughly formed; she fails to grasp the complete picture. When Godfrey tells her he is penniless, she rejoices; they are equals now, she tells him. But Godfrey replies that education, birth, and social prejudice will continue to separate them. It is impossible, he says, to marry into the peasantry. Mary's reaction to this, erupting from class and sexual repression, is violent.

Mingling between classes is seldom successful in Mrs. Moodie's world. Godfrey abandons Mary in spite of his obvious attraction. And when Anthony meets his old nurse Ruth after many years, the conversation is more sentimental than genuine; their speech is stilted, confined to the subject of an old dog, and the meeting ends lamely with Ruth hinting to Anthony that she is in need of money. *Jane Redgrave* is another story of the mingling of classes and its resulting problems. Jane herself, though educated, is a child of a mixed class marriage. Even though she is the parson's daughter, she is forced to sweep the floor and milk the cows. When she meets a handsome stranger and is told that he is from a wealthy family, she says automatically, "how impossible it will be for us to remain friends."[4] Rose too suffers from class dislocation; she is snatched from a country cottage. Her name is changed to Rosamond and she is tutored in city manners and urged to wear corsets. Her social veneer leads her to near destruction as she discovers the civilized vices of cunning and cruelty.

In Canada where servants and masters shared very close quarters, it must have troubled Mrs. Moodie more than a little to maintain what she considered to be an appropriate distance. But even in times when her own labour was identical to theirs and when she had no friends close by, she refused to sit at the table with her servants. And when Malcolm, the long-staying and unwelcome guest, taunted, teased, and flirted with the servants, she remonstrated with him. Servants will not respect their masters, she tells him, if they are not themselves respected within their position. One of Roland Massingham's many faults was his familiarity with servants; and when, in a fit of arrogance, he tells the coachman Jacob that he is his master, the servant tells him with true republican fervor, "You are no master of mine" (RM 19).

Despite her self-imposed separation from them, many of Mrs. Moodie's stories turn on the activities of her servants; indeed, for many years she had little other regular human contact. But it is a measure of her class consciousness that servants generally figure in her anecdotes in a humourous and stereotyped way. Her best sketches — those of Brian and Malcolm, for instance — involve beings of somewhat higher birth and greater education. It is as though she cannot take seriously the idea of complexity in the lower orders.

Of course, mixing with the working class cannot have been easy for one of Mrs. Moodie's conditioning. Flora Lindsay, a character clearly based on Mrs. Moodie herself,[5] when called upon to shake hands, performed "with very bad grace, for she had not as yet been seasoned by a long residence in a semi-democratic country" (FL 177). But Mrs. Moodie, in the seclusion of her Canadian existence, admits that mixing between classes added zest to life (LC 53).

A meeting between two distinct classes usually announces a comic episode. Thus, at Niagara Mrs. Moodie observes the following scene:

> Two young ladies, not of a highly educated class, were engaged in a lively conversation with two dashing English officers, who, for their own amusement, were practicing upon their incredulity. . . .
>
> (LC 357)

She often sets up encounters between gentlefolk and the uncultivated as in her story in which a gentleman shares a boat cabin with an uneducated American who appropriates his toothbrush. The gentleman, leagues ahead in manners and in trickery, then uses the brush for his toenails. The American, in response, has the delicacy to become sick. The story is told not so much because it belittles a man lacking in manners, but because it is an amusing incident told for its own sake. Nevertheless the social structure shows through and, in fact, gives the story its viability.

But class distinction was more than a comical matter to Mrs. Moodie; class hatred was a force of enormous magnitude. In the charivari chapter in _Roughing It in the Bush_ she enters into a long discussion of the social structure, opening the chapter with a discussion on servant problems and closing with a story involving the treatment of servants, an example of her frequent coupling of theory with example. She has, she explains, discovered the reason why American and English working class people hate those in her level of society: The hatred is the result of generations of pent up frustration from being held in a condition of almost total bondage. In the New World where a servant can leave at any time for other employment, he lashes out at the class which once held him in bondage. Mrs. Moodie can sympathize with this attitude in the abstract, although she is very often wounded in the concrete. In the balance, though, she claims that she values the Canadian servant more highly than the English for, freed from bondage, any affection between servant and master must be genuine. "It is a glorious country for the labouring class . . ." she says (LC 145).

Warfare between classes is something that Mrs. Moodie takes for granted. Education and personal advantage inspire hatred among the less privileged. When the Harford family in *Waiting for Dead Men's Shoes* is in danger of losing their wealthy uncle's money, the villagers secretly cheer at their misfortune. Mrs. Joe reflects the same attitude, rejoicing to see Mrs. Moodie actually working with her hands, in this case washing by hand some baby garments. Mrs. Moodie confesses she has never done such a thing before and hardly knows how to begin. She admits she does it badly, and for once she takes no pride in her ignorance. This story is, in fact, a turning point in Mrs. Moodie's attitude toward the types of skills which make for survival in the new land. Not that she herself announces this as a watershed experience, but it is at this juncture that her bitterness towards her neighbours softens and she sees them thereafter as less of a threat; they become for her curiosities who, for all their ignorance, have mastered the practical aspects of bush life.

The importance which Mrs. Moodie places on birth can be seen by the fact that she seldom introduces an important character without paying careful attention to his antecedents. Roland Massingham's father is presented by the line, he "kept a large wholesale stationers' shop in which he had amassed a fine fortune" (RM 35). Malcolm, Mrs. Moodie's unwelcome guest, might have been even less welcome had he not been the son of a Knight Companion of the Bath. Brian, the still-hunter, claims to have been "respectably born and educated, and had seen something of the world . . ." (RB 126). When he brings a gift of milk for the baby, Mrs. Moodie says it was with "the courtesy of a gentleman — or a man of benevolence and refinement" (RB 125). His madness, which might have frightened her in one less well born, was tolerable in gentlemanly shape. John E_____, a great favourite of Mrs. Moodie, is also introduced in the context of his family. In contrast, the servants in Mrs. Moodie's Canadian books seem to pop out of nowhere, Jenny perhaps being the single exception.

59

Genteel poverty, Mrs. Moodie seems to feel, always requires an accompanying covering statement. The old world culture considered poverty to be close to sin; and Mrs. Moodie always explains, almost in the same breath as she introduces a character, the reason for his economic condition. The Harfords in *Wating for Dead Men's Shoes* are scarcely presented when Mrs. Moodie plunges into the story of how the dead Captain, who had belonged to a good family, was unfortunately the youngest son and, therefore, without an income. Mrs. Wildegrave in *Mark Hurdlestone* is poor because her husband was hanged in the rebellion of 1745 for his mistaken loyalties. Other characters, having married for love, have forfeited property. Agnes Fitzgibbon, in her Introduction to Catherine Parr Traill's *Pearls and Pebbles*, reiterates the Strickland belief that poverty was a disgrace, and even suggests that the Strickland sisters married late because the shame of their poverty forced them to retreat for most of their young womanhood to Reydon Hall.[6]

Mrs. Moodie considers it a great irony that a man who appears to be a gentleman, and indeed is the son of a gentleman, is one of the worst criminals in the Kingston penitentiary. And in the insane asylum at Toronto she marvels at those who have lost their sense of social placement. A low-born woman fancies herself to be Queen Victoria; a well-born gentleman who once practised law is now confined with the rabble. This renunciation of class strikes Mrs. Moodie's sense of irony, and she is both amused and puzzled by it.

She herself never willingly surrendered what she considered to be her place. Working in the fields was not for Mrs. Moodie so much an abandonment of her femininity as a break in the social pattern. Only the most common women worked in the fields, and when necessity forced her to join them, she obeyed Providence by accepting her duty to her husband and to poverty, that "hard taskmaster" (RB 167). Typically she feels this descent had some enobling value in that she was able to reinforce herself as a dutiful wife and child of God: "The independent in soul can rise above the seeming disgrace of poverty, and hold fast to their integrity" (RB 167). This independence, which she clearly believed she possessed, permitted her to work without actually becoming one of the menial hands.

Her years in the bush with their deprivation and harsh realities undoubtedly softened her social concept. Jenny, with whom she spent all of one winter, became more of a friend than a servant, and achieves a larger degree of individuality than the other servants Mrs. Moodie describes. Speaking about the winter of 1837 she remarks that one must become poor to appreciate the better qualities of the poor; then they may be recognized as the brothers they are.

But the chasm between reality and romanticism persisted, and again and again Mrs. Moodie demonstrates her ambivalence about the working class. Near Montreal she watches a man drown. There is an unsuccessful but dramatic rescue attempt by a sailor, and Mrs. Moodie comments that "Such acts of heroism are common in the lower walks of life. Thus, the purest gems are often encased in the rudest crust, and the finest feelings of the human heart are fostered in the chilling atmosphere of poverty" (RB 41). And mingling between classes is not always damaging. In *Life in the Clearings* she remarks:

Balls. . .on public days. . .are composed of very mixed company, and the highest and lowest are seen in the same room. They generally contrive to keep to their own set — dancing alternately — rarely occupying the floor together. It is surprising the good will and harmony that presides in these mixed assemblies. As long as they are treated with civility, the lower classes show no lack of courtesy to the higher.   (LC 88f)

Visiting the Ontario village of Northport she is puzzled but admiring about its democratic aspects:

The distinctions, unavoidable among persons of wealth and education, are hardly felt or recognized here. Everyone is a neighbour in the strictest sense of the word, and the high and low meet occasionally in each other's house. Even

61

the domestics are removed by such a narrow line of demarcation, that they appear like members of one family.

(LC 160)

In Northport, Mrs. Moodie continues, an old captain lives, one of "nature's gentlemen" who, without benefit of an education, is wise, philosophical, and gifted in conversation.

The route to class mobility, Mrs. Moodie felt, was education. In the old order, education was not a necessity, and Mark Hurdlestone deliberately refused a university education, preferring to let money speak for his merits. But education in the New World was capable of interrupting the social pattern and even overcoming questionable blood. Marcella DeTrueba, a beautiful quadroon in *Richard Redpath*, is salvaged from her rank in society by the intervention of Mrs. Ingate, a cultivated Englishwoman who taught her both learning and morality. In an "Historic Footnote" in the *Victoria Magazine* Mrs. Moodie ecstatically describes Cardinal Wolsey's rise from the working classes.

> . . . the master spirit of his age . . . a man of the people, one of those wonderful men, arisen from the lower classes . . . to become a living witness of the intellectual power which nature impartially bestows, alike upon the peasant and the prince . . .[7]

Clement's sister Annie in the story *Wating for Dead Men's Shoes* surprises Rosamond by her drawing accomplishments. Annie explains the aberration by remarking that she was instructed in cultural accomplishments by a more highly placed relative.

Writing in the *Victoria Magazine*, Mrs. Moodie exhorts Canada to educate her sons. The rich should not fear that they will be less well served because the poor are educated. "A poor man who knows duty will serve better."[8] She even participated in the education of the working poor, editing with her husband the *Victoria Magazine* which had as its purpose the circulation of polite literature among the working class.

Education might soften class lines, but race hardened them, at times all but cancelling out other traditional barriers. Mrs. Moodie's pride in her own race is based on its accomplishments in government and in art; all other races fail in comparison. She does, however, admit that the English are arrogant and ignorant about Canada. Toward the Irish, whom she believed to be ignorant and unquestioning, she is generally patronizing. French Canadians only occasionally enter Mrs. Moodie's experience, and when they do she sees them picturesquely as handsome, lithe, active as "wild cats" (LC 27), with a careless disregard for danger; they are gay, light-hearted children who work all day and drink all night. Toward the Americans she is sometimes admiring, but once she refers to them as "gold-worshippers" because they permit their part of Niagara Falls to be used for industrial purposes; this is a surprising comment since Mrs. Moodie tends to admire engineering feats.

When she visits the penitentiary Mrs. Moodie asks which country produces the most criminals. Her first guess, which she does not record (probably Irish) is wrong, and she is informed that the majority of the prisoners are French Canadians or "men of colour" (LC 214). Next in order are the Irish, English, and Americans. Although there are a few Scots, she is told that they are the worst. The runaway slaves cause a great problem, and Mrs. Moodie supplies an anecdote aimed at "those who laud the black man and place him above the white . . ." (LC 214).

In *Richard Redpath* Mrs. Moodie portrays blacks and mulattoes as being almost invariably fat, gaudily dressed, and coarse, but possessed of a compensating generosity of spirit. Richard, though, disguised as a black, sees through the hypocrisy of race when he realizes that Betsey will not really look at him as a man until he has washed off his black paint. In this story the blacks and the Jew, Benjamin Levi, weave in and out, adding colour and character, but the circle of Anglo-Saxons is self-contained, and superiority is assumed as a right. Even Marcella is reminded to be humble because of the "drop of colour" in her blood. In *Life in the Clearings* Mrs. Moodie lingers over her description of the black waiters at the hotel in Niagara. "There were a dozen of these blacks in attendance, all of them young, and some, in spite of their dark colouring, handsome, intelligent looking men" (LC 349). The suggestion of intelligence appears to place a strain on Mrs. Moodie's credulity, but plainly she is curious rather than maligning in her feeling.

She was, of course, burdened with the racial attitudes of her time. Jewishness she automatically links with iniquity, and in describing Mark Hurdlestone she comments on the Jewish cast of his features. Josiah Spires, the Jewish boy in *Roland Massingham*, is calm, intelligent, and handsome, but he is picked out by Roland to be a victim. From victim he becomes informer, thus reducing the sympathy of the reader, and Mrs. Moodie is remarkably casual toward this innocent target of schoolyard cruelty. One wonders whether she has not selected a Jewish victim in order to minimize Roland's crime, a crime for which he himself is less than remorseful.

When two racial myths meet, Mrs. Moodie becomes confused, hardly knowing which to accept. This dual attitude is particularly apparent in her approach to the Canadian Indian. She is an eloquent admirer of the native people, and unlike many of her contemporaries, she seldom refers to them as savages. Their cunning, she says, springs from necessity rather than malice. Her admiration is sometimes uncompromising: the Indians "never" lie, "never" flatter, "never" forget a kindness. Their worst traits are those they share with wild animals of the forest. And yet Mrs. Moodie is clearly torn between the myth of the noble savage and the reality of her own observations. Her strict affirmatives are, in fact, closely followed by contradictory examples: "An Indian is Nature's Gentleman — never familiar, coarse or vulgar," she says,[9] and yet she presents Indians who are sullen, ugly, ungrateful, and who presume on her time by demanding that she make portraits of them.

Mrs. Moodie's conception of the Indian appears to arise from her Wordsworthian respect for the child in man and her feeling that the Indian is part of nature as are the fox and deer. But the

64

experience of having Indian neighbours forces her to frequent equivocation. Even so she never denies the Indian's inherent dignity. Just as she never thoroughly revises her social views, neither does she successfully sort out her racial feelings. Alternately enchanted and disenchanted, she moves from encounter to encounter, revising as she goes along.

In the closing chapter of *Life in the Clearings* Mrs. Moodie makes what she believes to be a final summary of her feelings on the subject of race and social structure, and it is a statement split with contradiction. Plainly she is baffled by the collision of social theory and the realities of human behaviour.

> That all men, morally speaking, are equal in the eyes of their Maker, appears to me to be a self-evident fact, though some may be called by His providence to rule and others to serve . . . Some Master spirit will rule, and the masses will bow down to superior intellect . . . We are advocates for equality of mind — for a commonwealth of intellect . . . But equality of station is a dream — an error which is hourly contradicted by reality . . . The rich and educated will never look upon the poor and ignorant as their equal.
>
> (LC 381 - 383)

Mrs. Moodie was never to see perfect equality in society, but she did acknowledge that it was possible in Canada to overcome the obstacle of low birth by hard work and education. The relatively shackling situation in England is only briefly referred to, and she never renounces her first allegiance to the land of her birth, nor does she criticize the English social structure. "The heart," she says, "acknowledges no other home than the land of its birth" (RB 37).

Mrs. Moodie herself sees that comparisons between England and Canada are unjust. "You cannot exalt the one at the expense of the other without committing an act of treason against both" (RB 30). And in *Roughing It in the Bush* she does attempt to avoid direct comparisons. It is only in her outbursts of homesickness that she touches on particular differences. What she does attempt in her first

65

Canadian book is to give the reader a true picture of life in the woods, and judging from the Cattermole lectures in England, people had often been given a false impression of the country. Canada was described in glowing terms in these lectures; the climate was played down; fruit, it was said, was so plentiful that it was given to hogs to feed on; the lakes "teem with white fish." [10] Mrs. Moodie was not alone in her sympathy for the gentleman immigrant. Joshua Fraser, in his book *Shanty, Forest and River Life* (1883), discusses the failure of these aristocratic settlers, their absurd keeping up of appearances which made serious inroads into their capital, and their vision of "estates" which never materialized. For some, he says, "immigration is simply carving out a home to starve in." [11]

In Mrs. Moodie's 1853 Introduction to *Life in the Clearings* she defends her stand that the backwoods of Canada was not a suitable home for educated people of the higher classes. But she also states some of the advantages of emigration, repudiating some of her former aristocratic conceptions, and acknowledging the healing of her homesickness.

The drive to emigrate seems to have operated for Mrs. Moodie as part of an economic law. In *Life in the Clearings* (Chapt. XVI) she discusses her notion of how the law of supply and demand operates. She mentions a question she has heard: what shall be done for fuel when all the firewood is burned? Her optimism in the face of this question is boundless, and when she proceeds to the problem of over-population she says:

> . . . it is but the natural means, employed by Providence to force the poorer classes, by the strong law of necessity, to emigrate and spread themselves over the earth, in order to bring into cultivation and usefulness its waste places.
>
> (LC 320)

As for what might happen when there are no longer any waste places, she has a quick reply. "When the world can no longer maintain its inhabitants, it will be struck out of being by the fiat of Him who called it into existence" (LC 320).

In Mrs. Moodie's Introduction to the first edition of *Roughing It in the Bush*, she sets out her belief that emigration is a necessity; indeed, it is an act of "severe duty" (xv). The purposes of emigration are first, to improve one's economical position; secondly, to escape the "sarcasm" of those who look down on the poor; and thirdly, to obey an impulse for the pursuit of independence. By this last point she means an escape from the social situation in which those who had been born to rule are denied, because of poverty, that right. Emigration was an elaborate but necessary method of face-saving, a gesture which expressed the wish to "forget the past and to live in the future" (RB xv).

The immigrant is successful, Mrs. Moodie says, if the will of God is followed. God has arranged that those who are used to rough ways and hard work will find independence and contentment. But those men and women of refinement and accomplishment will find only despair because they have not followed God's plan. These gentlemen settlers who figure so largely in her work were landless and without income because they were unlucky enough to be the second or third sons in their families in a day when only the first son inherited. Their dilemma is solved by Mrs. Moodie's simple formula: emigration. Again and again she reiterates that the reason for emigration is to escape the contempt of a society which places all its value on wealth. By emigration, a young man might make a fortune, then return home to live at his social station. Algernon, the disinherited son in *Mark Hurdlestone*, goes to India for just that reason, calculating that it would take him ten years to build up a large enough fortune to enable him to return and marry. Other emigrations are undertaken in a more permanent context and with an almost Christian sense of renewal. Robert and Richard Redpath, the sons of a ruined merchant, journey to Jamaica in order that they may become independent gentlemen. They even go through a sort of baptism in the shock of their shipwreck, although this sort of symbolism in Mrs. Moodie's work is more likely to be accidental than intentional. George Harford in *Waiting for Dead Men's Shoes* had lived all his life in the expectation of inheriting from his uncle. When that failed, his sister Caroline suggests that he emigrate as a

67

way out of his social predicament. In Canada, Caroline says, class is based on education alone.

The novel *Flora Lindsay* discusses in detail the philosophy of emigration. The book opens with an altercation between Flora and her husband, and Flora cries out, "Emigration is a terrible word, John, I wish it could be expunged from our *English* dictionary" (FL 6). When her husband explains that they will be poverty-ridden if they don't emigrate, she wails, "I would rather live in a cottage in England upon brown bread and milk than own a palace on the other side of the Atlantic" (7). Later she allows herself to be convinced and says to her neighbour Mrs. Ready, "Emigration . . . is a matter of necessity, not of choice" (22). Certainly this was Mrs. Moodie's point of view, although she confuses the issue in the charivari chapter by saying that "We were not compelled to emigrate" (RB 137).

Clearly Mrs. Moodie was unresolved for much of her life about the wisdom of her own decision to emigrate. Like Flora, of course, she had only limited control over her destiny. Her intense nineteenth century patriotism made the parting from her homeland painful, and the loss of caste in the New World caused her at least temporary suffering. Although she never returned to England, in a sense she never left. Her social obligations have all the reservations, contradictions, and circumlocutions of a woman whose philosophical position wavered between romanticism and realism and whose attachment shifted from one side of the Atlantic to the other. Politically she was caught between aristocratic instincts and the visible working out of republican ideals. Her social view, neither admirable nor dishonourable, expressed alarm at the speed of reform but championed such liberal causes as the abolition of slavery. Her view is valuable precisely because, like many others of her age, she was the voice of the concerned middle, trying to look in both directions at once and attempting, with fairness and intelligence, to reconcile a fragmented world.

NOTES

1. Susanna Moodie, *Life in the Clearings*, ed. Robert L. McDougall (Toronto: Macmillan, 1966), p. xvii.

2. Margaret Atwood, *The Journals of Susanna Moodie* (Toronto: Oxford University Press, 1970), p. 62.

3. Susanna Moodie, The *Victoria Magazine*, No. 3, 71.

4. The *Literary Garland*, Montreal (Jan.-Dec. 1848), 50.

5. There are numerous similarities between Mrs. Moodie and her heroine Flora Lindsay. Both were young English gentlewomen, both lived in a small coastal village in the east of England, both were married to men named John who were half-pay officers, veterans of the Napoleonic wars. Both had one child, a daughter, when the prospects of emigration presented itself, and both sailed to Canada on ships named the *Anne*. And aside from these similarities of detail, the personalities of the two women are remarkably alike: they are both romantic, adventurous, and sensitive women, and both of them, while resisting the idea of emigration, adapt themselves to the wills of their husbands.

6. Catherine Parr Traill, *Pearls and Pebbles* (Toronto: William Briggs, 1894), p. xvi.

7. Susanna Moodie, The *Victoria Magazine*, No. 1, 12.

8. *Ibid.*, No. 4, 90.

9. Susanna Moodie, *Roughing It in the Bush* (London: Richard Bentley, 1852), p. 46.

10. William Catermole, *Emigration. The Advantages of Emigration to Canada.* (1831: rpt; Toronto: Coles, 1970), p. 11.

11. Joshua Fraser, *Shanty, Forest and River Life* (Montreal: John Lovell and Sons, 1883), p. 109.

CONCLUSION

Energy, perhaps, more than originality was Susanna Moodie's strength. Her children's stories have none of the fantasy and warmth which is commonly associated with that genre today; she concentrated instead on the prevailing formula of translating youthful wilfulness into moral responsibility, sometimes, as in *The Little Prisoner*, producing epics tinged with sadism. Her novels such as *Mark Hurdlestone* and *Jane Redgrave* have all the marks of the potboiler: multi-generation plots, stories within stories, astounding coincidences, and an almost total detachment from reality. *Marital Speculations*, particularly the story *Waiting for Dead Men's Shoes*, has something of a Jane Austen touch in its self-contained domesticity; but the three stories suffer from Mrs. Moodie's clumsy attempt to marry social theory to romance, and the characters, almost without exception, are ill-conceived allegorical puppets. Mrs. Moodie's fiction has little to recommend it, in fact, except perhaps as an indication of what people in the mid-nineteenth century read for mild escape, the sort of fiction which, as Mrs. Moodie put it, one might turn to on a rainy afternoon.

But her fiction is of interest as a background to her Canadian books, *Roughing It in the Bush* and *Life in the Clearings*; and a thematic study of her fictional work isolates and defines those aspects of Mrs. Moodie's own personality which she was otherwise reluctant to disclose. Her interest in complex personality, consistently cloaked in pantheistic euphoria, declares itself as her major concern, and her unconscious reversal of sexual roles sheds more than a little doubt on her acceptance of convention. The contrarities of her social views undermine even her most ringing declarations. These three themes, the complex personality, sexual reversal, and the social structure, reveal something of the person behind the author, the human voice behind the benign assured persona who provided her "dear readers" with the promise of an afternoon's diversion.

The revelation of Mrs. Moodie's own personality appears only occasionally in her fiction, and then it is virtually invisible unless looked at under the magnifying glass of a thematic study. But in her Canadian books that personality moves to the foreground, making an insistent cry for recognition. Mrs. Moodie becomes the new variety of romance heroine, the pilgrim who must cope with a new habitat, what Carl Klinck calls a "modern knight," a person "seeking a way to live in the midst of social dislocation, philosophical nullity, economic slavery, decline of wealth, or impending deterioration" (RB xiv). As in her fiction this personality is revealed through her major themes; the only difference is that in her Canadian books Mrs. Moodie makes the move from romance into the more open fields of reality where she becomes more easily recognizable, more forceful, and more deserving of serious study.

Her three major recurring themes — the complex personality, sexual reversal, and the social structure — occur in all her works from her earliest children's tales to her most mature book, *Life in the Clearings*. And it is possible, if one looks at her works chronologically, to see in which direction these three themes change with time. The complex character appears only intermittently in her early fiction — in William Mathews, for instance, or Benjamin Levi or Wilhelmina Carr — in those persons whose eccentricity is dramatic or humourous and, in most cases, detached from the direct line of her narrative. Later, however, Mrs. Moodie produces the character Flora Lindsay whose individuality takes the form not of surface decoration, but of an inner independence of spirit. Brian in *Roughing It in the Bush* has the same sort of complexity, a pool of independence within his ocean of madness. Malcolm's multitude of aberrations almost, but not quite, succeeds in hiding what Mrs. Moodie admired in him, his inexplicable spasms of kindness and a reservoir of intelligence. Her own personality expanded against the Canadian landscape and gradually deepened in perception. Bending to social and economic pressure as well as tragedy, Mrs. Moodie struggled within herself for balance and arrived at a state of realism far removed from the bucolic romanticism of her early heroine Jane Redgrave.

71

Sexual reversal, almost certainly an unconscious conception, is seen in all her work, even in the children's stories in which the mature female figure automatically assumes the role of moral guide. The men in her Canadian books, at least those men of sensibility, are doomed to failure; women, on the other hand, endure even when they fail to succeed. As in her theme of complex personality, Mrs. Moodie's use of sexual reversal follows a path from romanticism to realism. The traditional romantic view of man as the swashbuckling hero and woman as the cherished, blushing maiden is reversed; women keep the fires going and the children fed while men miss boats, lose jobs, squander fortunes, abdicate their positions in the family, and fail to win the respect of society.

The social structure as perceived by Susanna Moodie also progressed from a fixed romantic view of lords, country vicars, and serving maids to a more realistic acceptance of a changing structure, so that in *Life in the Clearings* she goes so far as to suggest that the working class does have real grievances and that education can redistribute the respect of society if not the power.

Her three major themes can be seen as a natural outgrowth of her life and times. It appears to have been her inclination to respond to people more that to nature, though she often hides her human concern in the folds of religion and mystery and in the rhetoric which is attached to that kind of response. An interest in personality and a respect for individuality were part of the sensibility of her time. And Mrs. Moodie responded, at least occasionally, to the early stirrings of interest in psychological behaviour.

Her own experience and that of her sisters gave her every reason to place her trust more firmly in the female than in the male sex. As an immigrant she must have seen that women took at least as great a risk as men, and that the distribution of work in frontier society was often shifted without regard to gender. Women supported each other, and in their husbands' absences they grew in independence. While never an advocate of such reforms as universal suffrage, Mrs. Moodie seems to have taken for granted the female's right to be happy.

As for her social views, she was not only born into a century of enormous social change, but she herself experienced several abrupt social jolts. In Canada she was a witness to the new radical democracy while still burdened with conflicting aristocratic instincts. Her social conditioning was tested daily in the new country, and it was inevitable that she should arrive at a posture of compromise.

Stylistically Mrs. Moodie's fiction is undistinguished. Her novels and tales are conventional in design and in rhetoric, and furthermore her writings show all the flaws of haste. Such stories as *Richard Redpath* demonstrate her lack of control and the absurdities of her plots. She might be any novelist of her time, anxious to meet deadlines and to fill as many pages as possible. Her Canadian books, though lurching from plain style to high rhetoric, at least suggest an individual participating voice. Her camera eye sees all; she devours information, consumes scenery, hungers for vignettes, and grasps at social manifestations. Partly this extraordinary sense of detail is the result of her conditioning as a writer, but it may also have been the response of a unique individual who spent a lifetime trying to fit her observations into a conventional pattern.

Although she cannot be said to be a consciously Canadian writer, Mrs. Moodie's work touches on some of the themes which were later to become a part of Canadian literature. Chief among these is her explosion of the Utopian myth in *Roughing It in the Bush*, a blunt refusal to applaud change for its own sake or to eulogize, as romantic, an empty landscape. The value she placed on order and restraint represents a departure from American revolutionary spirit; it was not paradise Mrs. Moodie was looking for, but an ordered community, a facsimile of that which she left behind. Mrs. Moodie made a conscious attempt to explain Canadian speech usages although she herself seemed unwilling to adopt them, and in the *Victoria Magazine* she apparently made an effort to find writers who were specifically Canadian. Nevertheless it is stretching a point to say that Mrs. Moodie embodied the Canadian ethos; her roots were in English literature, and her mature life was lived mainly in pre-Confederation Canada when national consciousness was neither defined nor encouraged.

She is better defined as a bridging figure, a woman whose consciousness spanned two continents, two cultures, two political philosophies. She is a writer whose three major themes indicate a struggle between romanticism and reality, between the old order and the new, between the tug of tradition and the pull of progress. It is just this position — that of a voice in the middle — which makes Mrs. Moodie an interesting literary subject and a valued figure in the study of Canadian literature.

BIBLIOGRAPHY

Atwood, Margaret. *Survival.* Toronto: Anansi, 1972.

Baker, Ray Palmer. *History of English-Canadian Literature to the Confederation.* Cambridge: Harvard University Press, 1920.

Ballstadt, Carl. "Susanna Moodie and the English Sketch." *Canadian Literature,* 51 (winter 1972), 32 - 37.

Bissell, Claude. "Letters in Canada: 1944, Fiction." *University of Toronto Quarterly,* 24 (April 1955), 257 - 267.

Boulton, D'Arcy. *"Sketch of His Majesty's Province of Upper Canada."* 1815; rpt. Toronto: Baxter Publishing Co., 1961.

Boyce, Gerald. *Historic Hastings.* Belleville: *Ontario Intelligencer Ltd,* 1967.

Brown, Mary M. *The Literary Garland (Index).* Toronto: Bibliographical Society of Canada, 1962.

"Canuck," A. *Pen Pictures of Early Pioneer Life in Upper Canada.* Toronto: William Briggs, 1905.

Cattermole, William. Emigration. The Advantage of Emigration to Canada. 1831: rpt. Toronto: Coles, 1970.

Cowan, Helen. *British Migration to British North America.* Toronto: University of Toronto Press, 1961.

Craig, John. *By the Sound of Her Whistle.* Toronto: Peter Martin, 1966.

Davies, Robertson. *At My Heart's Core.* Toronto: Clarke Irwin, 1950.

Delefosse, F.M. ed. *Centenary History, St. John's Church, Peterborough 1827 - 1927.* Peterborough: The Renfrew Press, 1927.

Dictionary of National Biography. London: Smith, Elder, 1894.

Eaton, Sara. *Lady of the Backwoods, A Biography of Catherine Parr Traill.* Toronto: McClelland and Stewart, 1969.

Edgar, Matilda, ed. *Ten Years of Upper Canada in Peace and War.* (The Ridout Letters). Toronto: William Briggs, 1890.

Fraser, Joshua. *Shanty, Forest and River Life in the Backwoods of Canada.* Montreal: John Lovell, 1883.

Gairdner, William D. "Traill and Moodie: Two Realities." *Journal of Canadian Fiction*, 2 (spring 1972), 35 - 42.

Geikie, John C. ed. *George Stanley* or *Life in the Woods.* London: Routledge, Warne and Routledge, 1864.

Guillet, Edwin. *Colbourg, 1798 - 1948.* Oshawa: Goodfellow Printing Co., 1948.

_____ *Early Life in Upper Canada.* Toronto: University Press, 1963.

_____ *The Great Migration, The Atlantic Crossing.* London: Thos. Nelson, 1937.

_____ *The Lives and Times of the Patriots.* Toronto: The Ontario Publishing Co., 1963.

_____ *Pioneer Travel in Upper Canada.* Toronto: University of Toronto Press, 1933.

_____ *Valley of the Trent.* Toronto: The Champlain Society, 1957.

Haight, Cannif. *Country Life in Canada Fifty Years Ago.* Toronto: Hunter and Rose, 1885.

Hewison, John. *Sketches of Upper Canada.* Edinburgh: Oliver and Boyd, 1821.

Hume, Blanche, *The Strickland Sisters.* Toronto: Ryerson, 1929.

Imperial Dictionary of Universal Biography, The. London: William Mackenzie, 1863.

Jameson, Anna. *Winter Studies and Summer Rambles.* Toronto: McClelland and Stewart, 1965.

Kirkland, Caroline. *A New Home - Who'll Follow?* 1840; rpt. New Haven: College and University Press, 1965.

Klinck, Carl F. "A Gentlewoman of Upper Canada." *Canadian Literature*, 1 (summer 1959), 75 - 77.

Langton, W.A. *Early Days in Upper Canada.* Toronto: Macmillan, 1926.

L'Estrange, The Rev. A.G., ed. *The Friendships of Mary Russell Mitford as Recorded in Letters from Her Literary Correspondents.* 2 vols. London: Bentley, 1882.

Literary Garland, The. Montreal, Vol. 11, Old Series (Jan. - Aug. 1840), *Geoffrey Moncton;* Vol. 11, New Series (Jan. 1844 - Dec. 1845), *Mildred Rosier;* Vol. VI, New Series (Jan. - Dec. 1848), *Jane Redgrave.*

MacDonald, R.D. "Design and Purpose." *Canadian Literature*, 51 (winter 1972), 20 - 30.

Magee, William H. "Local Colour in Canadian Fiction." *University of Toronto Quarterly*, 28 (Jan. 1959), 176 - 189.

McCourt, Edward A. "Roughing It with the Moodies." *Masks of Fiction.* ed. A.J.M. Smith. Toronto: McClelland and Stewart, 1961, 81 - 114.

McTaggart, John. *Three Years in Canada.* London: H. Colburn, 1829.

Mickel, W.C. *City of Belleville History.* Picton: *Picton Gazette*, 1943.

Moir, John S. "Four Poems on the Rebellion of 1837." *Ontario History*, 57 (March 1965), 47 - 52.

Moodie, J.W. Dunbar. *Scenes and Adventures as a Soldier and Settler During Half a Century.* Montreal: Subscription printed by John Lovell, 1866.

_____ *Ten Years in South Africa.* London: Bentley, 1835.

Moodie, Susanna. *Enthusiasm and Other Poems.* London: Smith, Elder, 1831.

_____ *Flora Lindsay, Passages in an Eventful Life.* London: Bentley, 1854.

_____ *Flora Lindsay, Passages in an Eventful Life.* New York: DeWitt, n.d.

_____ *Geoffrey Moncton.* New York: DeWitt, 1855.

_____ *George Leatrim.* Edinburgh: Hamilton, 1875.

_____ *Life in the Clearings.* London: Bentley, 1853.

_____ *Life in the Clearings.* 2nd ed. ed. Robert McDougall. Toronto: Macmillan, 1959.

_____ *The Little Black Pony and Other Stories.* Philadelphia: Collins, 1850.

_____ *The Little Prisoner* or *Passion and Patience; and Amndment.* London: Dean, 1828.

_____ *Mark Hurdlestone, the Gold Worshipper.* London: Bentley, 1853.

_____ *Mark Hurdlestone, the Gold Worshipper.* New York: DeWitt, n.d.

_____ *Matrimonial Speculations.* London: Bentley, 1854.

_____ *The Monctons.* London: Bentley, 1856.

_____ *Profession and Principle.* London: Dean, 1833.

_____ *Roland Massingham* or *I Will Be My Own Master.* London: Dean, 1837.

_____ *Roughing It in the Bush.* 2 vols. London: Bentley, 1852.

_____ *Roughing It in the Bush.* New York: DeWitt, 1852.

_____ *Roughing It in the Bush.* New York: George P. Putnam, 1852.

———— *Roughing It in the Bush*. Toronto: Hunter, Rose and Co., 1871.

———— *Roughing It in the Bush*. Toronto: Bell and Cockburn, 1913.

———— *Roughing It in the Bush*. Toronto: McClelland and Stewart, 1923.

———— *Roughing It in the Bush*. Abridged and edited by E.W. Tichner. London: Thomas Nelson, 1932.

———— *Roughing It in the Bush*. Upper Saddle River, N.J.: Literature House, 1970. (Reprint of Putnam edition, 1852).

———— *Roughing It in the Bush*. ed. Carl Klinck. Toronto: McClelland and Stewart, 1962.

———— *Roughing It in the Bush*. Unabridged. Toronto: Coles, 1974.

———— *The Soldiers' Orphan; or Hugh Latimer*. London: Dean, 1853.

———— *Sparticus*. London: Newman, 1822.

———— *The World Before Them*. 3 vols. London: Bentley, 1868.

Morris , Audrey. *Gentle Pioneers*. 1968; rpt. Don Mills, Ont.: Paper Jacks, 1973.

Partridge, Florence. "The Stewarts and the Stricklands, The Moodies and the Traills." the *Ontario Library Review*, 40 (Aug. 1956), 179 - 181.

Poole, Thomas W. *A Sketch of the Early Settlement and Subsequent Progress of the Town of Peterborough*. 1867; rpt. Peterborough: The *Peterborough Review*, 1941.

Pope-Hennessy, Una. *Agnes Strickland, Biographer of the Queens of England*. London: Chatto and Windus, 1940.

Purdy, A. "Atwood's Moodie." *Canadian Literature*, 47 (winter 1971), 80 - 84.

Radcliff, The Rev. Thomas, ed. *Authentic Letters from Upper Canada.* Toronto: Macmillan, 1953.

Roy, Jennet. *History of Canada for the Use of Schools.* Montreal: Armour and Ramsay, 1847. (Favourably reviewed by Mrs. Moodie in the first issue of the Victoria Magazine.)

Scott, Lloyd M. "The English Gentlefolk in the Backwoods of Canada." *Dalhousie Review,* 39 (spring 1959), 56 - 57.

Strickland, Agnes. *Lives of the Queens of England.* Revised Edition. London: Longmans, Green, Reader and Dyer, 1875.

Strickland, Jane. *Life of Agnes Strickland.* Edinburgh: Wm. Blackwood and Sons, 1887.

Strickland, Samuel. *Twenty-Seven Years in Canada West* or *The Experience of an Early Settler.* 1853; rpt. Tokyo: Charles E. Tuttle, 1970.

Sutherland, Ronald. *Second Image.* Toronto: New Press, 1971.

Thomas, C. "Happily Ever After." *Canadian Literature,* 34 (autumn 1967), 43 - 58.

Thomas, C. "Journeys to Freedom." *Canadian Literature,* 51 (winter 1972), 11 - 19.

Traill, Catherine Parr. *The Backwoods of Canada.* London: C. Knight, 1836.

———— *Canadian Crusoes.* London: A. Hall, Virtue, 1859.

———— *The Canadian Settlers' Guide.* Introduction by Clara Thomas. McClelland and Stewart, 1969.

———— *Pearls and Pebbles.* Toronto: Wm. Briggs, 1894.

———— *The Young Emigrants.* 1899; rpt. New York: Johnson, 1969.

Victoria Magazine, The. Sept. 1847 - Aug. 1848; rpt; Vancouver: University of British Columbia Press, 1968.

80

Weaver, E.P.W. *Canadian Magazine*, 48 (March 1917), 473 - 476.

Woodcock, George. Editorial. *Canadian Literature*, 51 (winter 1972), 3 - 10.